To Linda
Thank you
for your support
& smile
Sumi.

goodbye mme. b.

sex, marriage and the modern japanese woman

CHIN MUSIC PRESS

fall 2007

CHIN MUSIC PRESS — *PUBLISHERS*

SEATTLE ✻ TOKYO

CHIN MUSIC PRESS INC.
2621 24th Ave. W.
Seattle, WA 98199
USA.

http://chinmusicpress.com
http://goodbyemadamebutterfly.com

FIRST {1} EDITION

Innards assembled & designed *by* Craig Mod (during the very, very rainy season)

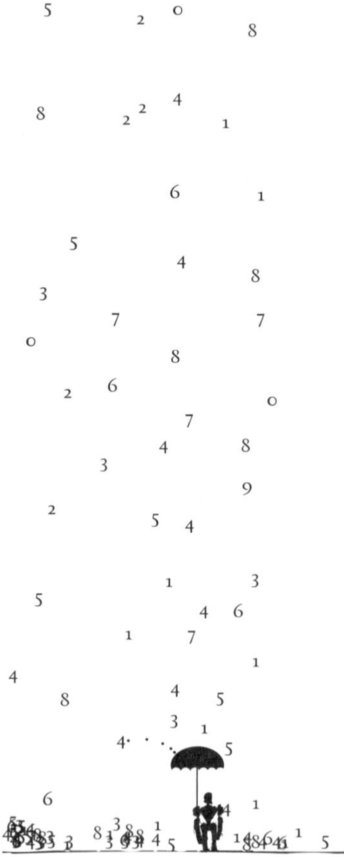

There are *Butterflies* and there are *Madames* (many modern ones congregating in Jiyūgaoka). There are also Madames duplicated and transposed in the manner of the symmetry of a Butterfly. And these Madames just might be saying goodbye to one another.

Printed and bound ever so tightly by the soft and loving hands at YUSHIN PRINTING in Tokyo, Japan.

G.M.B. TRANSLATION CREDITS

Washoi!, Red Circles, Purgatory, The Fix:
Yuko Enomoto

Joint Venture, Me, the Yin Yang Master & the Triple Sheep, The Shinto Priest's Wife, Long Distance Love:
Yuko Enomoto & Bruce Rutledge

Synchronicity, The Mannequin, The Sex Volunteer:
Sumie Kawakami

LIBRARY OF CONGRESS CATALOGING-IN-PUBLICATION DATA

Goodbye Madame Butterfly:
Sex, Marriage and the Modern Japanese Woman
by Kawakami, Sumie

translated by Yuko Enomoto; edited by Bruce Rutledge; designed by Craig Mod; copyedited by David Rutledge

ISBN 978-0974199535

1. Asian Studies
2. Cultural Studies 3. Women's Studies
4. Japanese Studies 5. Sociology
6. Astrology

Also by Sumie Kawakami (川上澄江):

Tsuma no Koi: Tatoe Furin to Yobarete mo (Wives in Love: Even if It Is Called Adultery), co-authored by Taro Ohata, published by Astra, 2003

Kuhaku & Other Accounts from Japan, contributing author, published by Chin Music Press, April 2005.

This book is dedicated to all the women who
shared their stories of life, sex and love with me.

PREFACE:

The women portrayed in *Goodbye Madame Butterfly* are real. I interviewed all of them between 2005 and 2007. I didn't put out any ads to find them; instead I tracked them down via word of mouth, one person leading me to another and then another until I found the stories contained in this book.

Many of the women I interviewed asked me variations of this question: "My life isn't all that interesting or exciting. My life is so ordinary. Are you sure you want to hear my story?" I told them that the fact that they volunteered to talk about love and their sex lives (or lack thereof) was a good indicator that they had something they wanted to express. And I was right. Everyone had an interesting story to share. We couldn't include all of them in this book due to space and time constraints, but I felt that each woman I talked to had something important to say. But before going into the book in detail, allow me to offer some pertinent background information.

Japan is known as a place where sexual fantasies come true. At least, that's the reputation. The sex industry is so prevalent in Japanese culture that it can influence even the most personal and intimate matters. Prostitution is illegal in Japan, but "entertainment and amusement" services, as they are called, continue unabated all over the country. A man can go to an establishment called *soapland*{1}, for example, and pay a "bath service fee" to have a woman wash him with soap. So-called *fashion health*{2} clubs offer genital massages, blow-jobs, hand-jobs and other sexual services. *Delivery health*{3} businesses deliver a woman — or women, if you so desire — straight to your door. And *image*

1 ソープランド (*soopurando*). Terms for most sex establishments in Japan are based on English words and rendered in the katakana syllabary used for borrowed words.

2 ファッションヘルス (*fasshyonherusu*). Sometimes referred to as just ヘルス (*herusu*).

3 デリバリーヘルス (*deribari-herusu*). Also known by the short version, デリヘル (*deriheru*).

clubs[1] allow people to dabble in costume play. Men can choose women dressed as nurses, teachers, playboy bunnies or characters from popular anime films. Strip clubs often encourage audience members to participate in the shows. And at *happening bars,*[2] as the name implies, sex has a way of just happening, whether it be with an acquaintance or a slew of strangers.

You don't have to travel deep into the inner sanctum of Japan's red light districts to find these places. The sex shops are often integral parts of their communities. Schoolchildren in Japan's urban centers commute through narrow streets lined with these clubs. There is no attempt to hide these establishments from view.

Japanese men generally are not shy about using these services, either. Middle-class men in business suits openly read pornographic stories in the sports newspapers while commuting from work in the evening. Japanese women, too, seem more lenient than North American women when it comes to men using these services. While I was researching this book, I often heard wives say they would forgive their husbands for cheating on them with a "professional" because that would be just about having sex, not becoming emotionally attached.

However, a striking paradox emerged in my research of this book: while the sex industry maintains a high profile in Japan, the nation doesn't seem to be having much actual sex. A case in point is the results of the Global Sex Survey by Durex,[3] the world's largest condom maker. In its 2005 survey, the company interviewed 317,000 people from forty-one countries and found that Japan ranked forty-first in terms of sexual activity. The survey found that people had sex an average of 103 times a year, with men (104) having more sex than women (101). The

1 イメージクラブ (*imeejikurabu*)

2 ハプニングバー (*hapuningubaa*)

3 http://www.durex.com/uk/files/2005_GGS%20Report_final.pdf

Japanese, at the very bottom, reported having sex an average of forty-five times a year.

Japan also ranked second to last, just ahead of China, in terms of sexual contentment. Globally, forty-four percent of all adults claimed to be happy with their sex lives, but only twenty-four percent of the Japanese and twenty-two percent of the Chinese said they were.

A survey conducted jointly by the Ministry of Health, Labor and Welfare and the Japan Family Planning Association also found that the number of "sexless couples" has increased over the years, with more than one-third of all married people in Japan classed as being "sexless." The survey, conducted in November 2006, was distributed to three thousand men and women between the ages of sixteen and forty-nine. It had a 51.9 percent response rate.

The survey uses the definition of "sexless couples" by the Japan Society of Sexual Sciences as couples who go without sexual contact for a month or longer for no specific reason. The survey found that 39.7 percent of respondents had not had sex for a month or longer. It also found that 34.6 percent of married Japanese people are sexless, about three percentage points higher than the previous survey conducted in 2004.

When asked why they are not having sex, nineteen percent said it was "tiresome." Another fourteen percent said sex had become one-sided after they had children. Thirteen percent said they had other things to do that were more fun than sex.

I knew about the trend toward sexless marriages before I started this book. Many of my female friends are in sexless relationships. When I asked them why they stopped having sex, they would tell me it was just a bother to do so — they then have to take a shower, wash the sheets, et cetera, and it is so much easier to just pretend to be asleep when their husband comes into the room. It reminds me a bit of people who don't like to cook because they hate cleaning up afterwards. Other women say they don't have time for sex because their husbands work late and often don't return until after midnight. Some of my friends even share rooms with their daughters and leave the main bedroom for the husband. The women say they sleep better this way.

So here is this country with a huge, thriving sex industry and an inordinate amount of sexless marriages. It would be easy to conclude that the men are leaving all their sexual energy behind in the soaplands and fashion health establishments. But that is just part of the story. What are the Japanese women doing in the meantime? Are they just waiting at home for their husbands? Are they secretly planning divorces?

It's clear that modern Japanese women are not just sitting around moping. In fact, *furin*,[1] or adultery, has been a buzzword of sorts since the late 1980s, after a popular TV drama focused on the healthier aspects of women having affairs. Adultery still is considered immoral in Japan. The very construction of the word — *fu* is a negative prefix, and *rin* means moral — makes that clear. But a double standard is at work. A common saying, said to have originated in the Edo Period, is that "affairs show a man's ability to generate money." Even in postwar Japan, adultery between married men and single women has always been part of the picture. On the other hand, it was illegal until 1947 for a married woman to have an affair. Violators — both the women and their lovers — could face up to two years in prison if the betrayed husband requested it.

When it emerged that more married women were having affairs, Japan's sex industry, including the enormous pornography sector, got to work. It created the myth of the horny housewife. Countless Internet sites feature lists of supposed housewives

1 不倫

waiting for sex. While many of these sites are doubtless scams, is there some truth to the stereotype of married women looking for sex? Do they enjoy cheating on their husbands? Does it give them a sexual thrill?

These are the questions I originally wanted to find answers to when I began interviewing women in 2003 for another book, in Japanese, that I co-authored with Taro Ohata. The theme of the book, entitled *Tsumanokoi: Tatoe Furin To Yobaretemo* (Wives in Love: Even If It's Called Adultery),[1] was to reveal the sexuality of married women who had cheated or were cheating on their husbands.

When I started out, I was worried that finding such women would be difficult. But through word of mouth, I was able to meet a sufficient number of married women who claimed that they had cheated on their husbands at least once. Most of them were in unhappy, sexless marriages, but they were unwilling to separate from their husbands out of concerns over their ability to support themselves financially and for the sake of their children. To my surprise, these women were extremely open about their experiences during the interviews. They almost seemed happy to tell their stories, despite the seemingly unhappy situations they were in. Here is how one of the women put it:

> *"I can only talk to one friend about my experience because I know that she is doing the same thing. We both feel safe talking about it. I could never discuss this with my other friends. It is not only because I am afraid of my husband finding out. I'm equally afraid that I would be severely criticized by my female friends, my sister, or especially my mother. No one would tolerate me if they found out I'm committing adultery."*

1 妻の恋—たとえ不倫と呼ばれても, published by Astra Inc.

Like this woman, many of the women I interviewed were tired of hiding in the closet: they needed to be listened to and they wanted their stories told. Yet they lacked the will to fix their broken relationships. In many cases, both parties agreed from the beginning that they would not intervene in each other's lives. But a relationship of convenience is doomed to be short-lived. Many women found themselves in a vicious cycle of finding a lover, breaking up with him and searching for a new lover to replace him.

This went on for a while, and I was getting sick of meeting all these "cheaters," when suddenly something clicked. I was talking on the phone to a married woman who kept bragging that she had a series of lovers. To be honest, I was getting a bit annoyed by her. I asked, absent-mindedly, what she was trying to achieve by continuing to do this. She suddenly burst out at me: "You sound just like my husband. Who do you think you are, asking me what I want to achieve? If I knew I wanted to achieve anything at all, I wouldn't have been so miserable to begin with!"

Startled, I asked her what I did wrong to hurt her feelings. She said she hated me for being overbearing and that I basically knew nothing about her suffering.

"But you can leave your husband if you want to. He is not keeping you chained, is he?" I protested.

"How can a divorced woman like you have a say about marriage and family? I do all I can to keep my family together," was her answer. She refused to cooperate with me any longer, requested that her story be deleted from my draft of the book and hung up on me. I tried to contact her again, but she never took my call or replied to my email messages.

I was left clueless. She was right about my not knowing anything about her suffering. There was little I could do except move on.

On another occasion, a woman shouted at me through tears in a coffee shop where I was interviewing her: "How can you tell me that I can just get out of my marriage? You may have worked all these years, but I haven't worked since my first child was born. How am I supposed to make a living?"

My first book came out in 2004. In it, I concluded that the image of horny wives desperate for juicy sexual encounters is a myth created by the media. The wives we interviewed had needs far beyond the physical. They wanted their lovers to fill their loneliness, emptiness and lack of self-worth. While some of these women said that through their adultery, they realized how deeply they loved their husbands, or how much their husbands loved them, most of them admitted that these affairs didn't make them happier. Worse, many said they found themselves even unhappier once the affair ended, due to their guilt and lack of self-worth. They want their husbands to love them and show them warmth. In many cases, having affairs may put their marital problems on hold temporarily, but it did not bring them solutions.

Although the book was generally well received, deep inside I knew something had gone wrong. I felt guilty for not being honest. During the interviews, some of these women were openly jealous of my role as a seemingly independent single mother without knowing the difficulties I faced. It hurt me when I heard them say, "What do you know about my unhappiness? You are one of the lucky ones who are blessed with professional skills, while most of us don't have that luxury."

This may have been a legitimate claim, given Japan's struggling economy back then. The employment situation for women is better nowadays, but women often lose a lot financially after a divorce, especially if they are not working. In 2003, single-mother households in Japan earned a little over two million yen (less than twenty thousand dollars) annually, much less than half the average income of a typical white-collar worker.[1] The average income of salaried workers in Japan with more than one year of working experience in 2003 was 5.44 million yen, according to the National Tax Agency. I realized that a woman's sexual and emotional life cannot be fully explained unless we analyze her social and economic environment.

Another issue I faced was my own prejudice. My professional pride prevented me from reacting aggressively toward comments about how I had it "easy." I wanted to yell at them that being financially independent is not as easy as they think, that I give it all I've got to work and raise my daughter, while they are sitting on their asses, moping.

Often these women wanted me to give them recognition, approval or sympathy. But I wasn't ready to offer any of these things, not so much because I was trying to stay objective as a journalist, but perhaps because of my personal/emotional issues: I was secretly jealous of their status as wives, their ability to maintain that position without financial worries, their ability to go out and satisfy their sexual desires. After all, I was coming out of a nasty divorce and was struggling to re-establish myself as a single mother back then. Having been cheated on many times by my ex, I wasn't in the mood to be sympathetic to these wives who enjoyed the luxury of not having to work, spending their time in nail salons, fancy shopping centers or luxurious cafés, and then going off and having sex while their husbands were at the office working hard to maintain the lifestyle they had grown accustomed to.

I covered all this up by trying to appear "objective." But I

1 Ministry of Health, Labor and Welfare, the national single mother household survey conducted in 2003, published in 2005: http://www.mhlw.go.jp/houdou/2005/01/h0119-1.html

knew that my anger revealed itself here and there. The harshest criticism came from a woman I admired. "What are you trying to achieve by writing this?" she asked. "Obviously, you are not supporting these women, yet you come short of criticizing them. Where do you stand? It looks to me that you are just making fun of them, like other male writers."

It was painful for me to admit my own shortcomings. This was around the time when my publisher, editor and long-time friend, Bruce Rutledge, asked me to expand on my interviews to write a book about the sexuality of Japanese women in general. That conversation took place three years ago. He and his wife, business partner and translator of this book, Yuko Enomoto, convinced me that such a book would be an eye-opener to Western readers. Although I was moved by their enthusiasm, I wasn't exactly sure how I could overcome the obstacles I faced in my previous project. While Bruce and Yuko said they enjoyed my interviews in my first book, our biggest challenge in *Goodbye Madame Butterfly* was providing some social, economic and historical background to these stories without interfering too much with my rather subjective writing style. Through trial and error, we gradually moved away from the idea of including statistics and lengthy explanations of Japanese society and the economy, and focusing more on the stories of these women. We believe that they speak for themselves. The more academic analysis must be tackled in another book.

Secondly, we agreed that rather than focusing on married women, the book would pull back and take in the lives of single and divorced women as well.

Thirdly, I decided that I would only write stories about women I like, respect and admire. I know this doesn't sound scientific at all, but through my bitter experience with my first book, I knew that I wasn't going to do a good job if I could not relate to my subjects. Surprisingly, by admitting my shortcomings, I also began to listen more carefully to the women I interviewed. I started to understand their stories in a deeper way. I won't pretend that I know how they feel, but I do believe that this collection shows both the weaknesses and strengths of modern Japanese women.

Fourthly, I decided not to try to wrap up each story and make conclusions about the lives of these women. Instead of looking for generalizations, I worked to get the details right. I tried to reconstruct their stories as faithfully as I could. Readers will find the women's version of the truth in these pages and can draw their own conclusions. In order to facilitate that process, we have created a companion website[1] with a forum for people who would like to discuss the issues raised in this book.

I fictionalized some parts of these stories to protect the identities of these women as well as their family members, friends and lovers. Some women told me that fictionalization was not necessary, but I still insisted that I make some alterations just to protect others who may be involved, since I had not spoken to any of those people and therefore had no permission to write about them.

Some of these women shared email messages or letters from their husbands or lovers without permission. Other than that, these stories are solely based on the women's versions of events. They are not substantiated. This was partly because interviewing their partners, lovers and others who may be involved in their stories was difficult. It was also because I felt that this wasn't my purpose in this book, which is supposed to be a collection of stories told by women. What do the men have to say? You will hear from a sex volunteer and the owner of a sex clinic,

1 http://goodbyemadamebutterfly.com

both interviewed for this book, but that is it. The men will have to wait for another book.

In order to make these stories ring true to the women I interviewed, I shared draft manuscripts with some of them when they requested it. Some of them tried to rewrite my scripts completely. In these cases, I had to negotiate with them word by word, until we came up with the words we both agreed on.

These stories were born out of collaboration between me and the women interviewed. The interviews were conducted over coffee and cake in the afternoon or over wine in the evening after work. Some of the women broke down and cried as they dug up difficult memories. Some became angry when I peppered them with questions, even to the extent of walking out on me. Still others kept sending email messages to my cellphone, giving me updates as if I were attached to these developments for life.

I questioned them, listened to their stories, nodded in approval, consoled them, cried over their tragedies, even scolded them when I felt it was necessary. I often shared my stories of love with them. Some became my friends, others walked out of my life after just one interview. I know that I broke a lot of rules taught in journalism school, and these stories may not be purely journalistic, but I still consider them to be true. After all, every story has multiple truths — it all depends on who is telling the story and who is listening.

S. K.
Tokyo, July 2007

Once upon a time, I dreamt I was a butterfly, fluttering hither and thither, to all intents and purposes a butterfly.

I was conscious only of following my fancies as a butterfly, and was unconscious of my individuality as a man.

Suddenly I awoke, and there I lay, myself again.

Now I do not know whether I was then a man dreaming I was a butterfly, or whether I am now a butterfly, dreaming that I am a man.

CHUANG-TZU
3rd century BC

WASHOI!

Chami, Bar Owner, 27

It's seven pm in Kabukicho and the neon is just beginning to flicker. Chami prepares her cozy, ten-seat bar for another night of revelry. The pub is in a corner of an anonymous multi-use building surrounded by happening bars, host clubs, sex-toy shops, cabarets and soaplands.

Chami, impeccably made up, readies the bar for its opening at eight. She will be serving customers until sunrise. Chami and three other friends own the bar, but she and Koriki are usually the ones in charge; when they get some time off, they visit other bars in the vicinity. Chami thinks that in spite of appearances, Kabukicho still has remnants of that close-knit downtown sort of feel.

Their business has increased greatly in the past six months. They're getting close to turning a profit. "What we've got here is a gathering space, a place everybody wanders into looking for fun, you know, a place you can meet somebody, have a good drink," Chami says. Regulars at Chami's bar are of all ages, sexual persuasions and professions. Her encounters here are what helps keep her going, she says.

Goods from Japanese festivals decorate the walls along with posters from the 1950s and antiques (including a statue of a kimono-clad couple, who from the top look like any ordinary pair, but view them from below to see their exposed genitals intertwined in an act of sex). Hip-hop tunes play in the background, and Disney charms hang from bottles that line the shelves. Chami and her friends wear uniforms — a festival shirt over a pair of jeans.

The four women are all friends from middle school. Though they have taken different paths in the fifteen or so years since they were classmates, they held one thing in common: a love of festivals, or *matsuri*, as they're known in Japan. They love shouting "*washoi!*"[1] while hoisting portable shrines, banging on the *taiko* drums and making general merriment.

But matsuri are traditional events, so when four women come together to get rowdy, they really stand out — and not in

1 A cheer given during a festival, like "heave ho!"

a good way. Female shrine carriers are rare, but when these four get in on the action, they do it with flair, shouting "Outta the way! Outta the way!" as they run the shrine through the streets. This irritates the men, who push back: "Women, get outta here!"

"It's none of your frickin' business!" Chami and her friends yell back.

"It's totally fun," Chami says. And the saké they drink afterwards tastes exceptionally good, she adds with a proud snort.

At the bar, Chami spikes her hair, dyed a golden brown, with wax and applies black eyeshadow, which makes her eyes pop out. Chami is generous with her laughter and speaks in a somewhat dated street lingo, but beneath this boisterous exterior is a sensitive soul who lost a young love when she was just twenty-one.

"It's been six years, but I don't talk about him to many people. I don't want people poking around. I only tell people who I think are OK. He died in December, just before his twenty-fifth birthday. He'd be thirty-one if he was alive," she says.

Chami met Kazuaki at a beauty salon while she was in high school. One day, he asked her to become a model for a haircut. She accepted, thinking it would be fun; that's how they began seeing each other. At the time they were just friends. Kazuaki became her boyfriend several years later.

Until the day that he died, Kazuaki was Chami's only true love. But through those years, their relationship was on-again, off-again mainly because of infidelities on either side.

"I fooled around a lot, so it went both ways. 'You're doing it so I'm doing it too.' That was my excuse at the time. Those women he went out with were psychotic. When I was with him, one came crashing into his place, another one kept calling and calling," Chami recalls.

"The girls always left things behind — make-up, pajamas. It's like they're saying, 'Hey, I was here, OK?' I used to wash the pajamas a girl left behind. Sound stupid? Yeah, but I couldn't just leave them there. One time while I was sleeping with Kazuaki, some girl tried to come in. She was bawling on the other side of the door. She'd yell, 'Who is it? Who's there with you?' She was making a huge fuss. I'm like, 'What the hell's going on? It's midnight!' and I open the door. 'Come in. Hey, Kazuaki, that girl's here again.' I sit them both down, serve some tea and say, 'You guys talk to each other. I'm outta here.' That happened all the time."

All the girls Kazuaki saw thought they were the only ones, but Chami knew about all of them — their names and their faces. Though he fooled around, she believed she was his one true love. "'Go fool around to your heart's content. Better now than after we're married,' you know? When it came to other girls, I didn't really make it a big deal. I was like, 'Do what you want. You'll figure it out some day.' But then sometimes the frustration would build up and I'd explode."

One day, Kazuaki showed up with a ring. He told Chami that he'd clean up his ways with the women, and things at work should settle down a bit. Please marry me, he said. Chami accepted.

But old habits die hard. Engagement didn't stop his womanizing overnight. Chami fooled around too — out of exasperation, she says — but when Kazuaki found out about it, he hit her.

"I can be sassy, so you can't blame him for hitting me. Kazuaki did karate, so he knew never to hit me in the face because it bruises. So he'd grab me by the hair and drag me around, or punch and kick me in the back or stomach. He was fooling around himself, but when I did it he got so pissed. He always hit me. But I never apologized. I just put up with it. It hurt but I never let it show. My dad was abusive, so in a strange sort of way, I am used to being hit."

After one of their many fights, Kazuaki called Chami and told her to come over.

"He called me and said, 'Come here now.' I was like, 'Why? I'm not going nowhere. I don't feel like it anyway.' That's what I said, but I wanted to see him so I went. As soon as I opened the door, he suddenly scooped me off the floor and held me real tight. 'I'm like, whoa, what's this?' Everything was back to normal. But then, I step into his room and it's full of stuff from other women, like, they were there right up until I showed up. I said, 'That's why I hate coming here.' We fought again and then I went home."

The next day Kazuaki died in a motorcycle accident. He drove home drunk and crashed.

Chami would learn about Kazuaki's death ten days later. Kazuaki had a quick temper that had landed him in jail a few times. In the beginning when he disappeared, Chami used to get very worried and call the detention centers looking for him. A person can only make one call from jail, and Kazuaki used to call the salon. Chami was reluctant to call the salon to find out which detention center had him, so she tried to track him down herself. Even then, the police never gave her a straight answer on the phone because she wasn't a relative. She had to go directly to the police station and ask if Kazuaki was incarcerated. There were only three or four places in the city where Kazuaki was likely to be held, so it was never too hard to find him. This time, however, they had just fought, and Chami was in no hurry to find him.

Ten days after Kazuaki died, Chami and Koriki were playing taiko drums at a festival. Chami ran into the owner of a bar she frequented and asked him, "My boyfriend's not here. Think he's in jail again?" Without anwering the question, he said, "Come to my bar after the festival." He told her to come with Koriki. She thought nothing of it at the time and just said, "Sure."

Chami was feeling great that day. The festival was a ball and after having a wild time, she headed to the bar with Koriki. Strangely enough, the bar was closed. The owner was seated at a table with his wife. Chami commutes by motorcycle, so he usually doesn't offer her a drink. But that day, he kept pushing drinks on her. Finally realizing there was something wrong, Chami asked, "What's going on?" Then the wife began to cry.

"Chami, you're a strong kid. Listen carefully. Kazuaki died ten days ago."

They talked about the accident, the seriousness of the wounds on his face and head and how the family quietly returned his body back to Wakayama Prefecture where they held a closed service. Kazuaki's affairs with numerous women left the family no choice but to refrain from contacting every single one of them. The wife told Chami that she really wanted to let Chami know first, but didn't have the courage. "I'm so sorry," she said, crying.

Koriki held Chami outside the bar as she cried.

"I didn't recover for a year," Chami recalled. "I was like a dead person. I couldn't stop crying. I couldn't do nothing. When I would come across stories like this in a movie or a blog or a book, it made me so mad. It was so fake. When I read stories about these women who felt sorry for themselves, like, 'I'm going to live the rest of my life thinking about this dead person,' I was like, that's bullshit. Even if the person you love dies, you still have sex with someone else, you still fall in love, that's human, you know? People aren't that pure; they're more jaded than that. OK, so maybe not everyone's like that, but I know I am. That got me really depressed one time."

Chami worked as a home care provider at the time. The serious nature of her work kept her on her feet. But when her work was over, she found that she would often shut off and think about suicide. "I was so mentally screwed up," Chami recalled. "If I wasn't careful, I acted suicidal. I keep thinking to myself, 'Go to the tracks, go to the tracks,' but I find myself stopping right before the train arrives. I tried slashing my wrists, but couldn't. I was too scared. That's it. In a way, you need some sort of momentum to commit suicide. It wasn't in me. People who commit suicide — they've got passion. I've tried to kill myself many times, but couldn't. That's me."

A FRIEND of Chami's from middle school had been running a bar in Koenji in western Tokyo, but he decided he wanted to travel overseas for a while. "Do you wanna try running it?" he asked Chami. "Sounds fun. I'll do it," she said and the decision was made.

Chami and her three best friends from middle school began operating the bar. Even though they were complete amateurs, they had fun running the little joint. It turned out to be difficult work, though.

"We just jumped into it without much thought," Chami said. "We were like, 'Hey, it'll all work out. We just have to show up. What's the big deal?' So in the beginning we were selling things at a loss."

The plan was to run this bar for one year. By the end of that one-year period, they were each able to draw a small monthly salary of about forty to fifty thousand yen a person. They had a lot of fun running the bar, but when one of the patrons talked to them about Miyakojima, a small island that was part of the Okinawa cluster of islands in the south, their wanderlust got the better of them and they closed the bar to travel.

Miyakojima has a subtropical ocean climate and stays comfortably warm throughout the year. The island is surrounded by coral and emerald blue waters. Tropical fish swim in the ocean. The friends rented a house and spent their days snorkeling, diving for clams and fishing for dinner. They'd pick herbs from the field and make tempura. They were living a nearly self-sufficient lifestyle, taking from nature's abundance. For three months, they lived on 100,000 yen and had pure, unadulterated fun.

When money began to run out, they returned to Tokyo to find work. "For about a month, we looked for a part-time job we could ditch, like, after a month or so, and just make a ton of money," said Chami.

She had another reason for returning to the island. At the time, Chami had fallen for a man from Miyakojima and promised to return to him after earning some money back in Tokyo. Kazuya was her first love since Kazuaki passed away.

❀

CHAMI HAD two possessions she always carried around with her: the engagement ring Kazuaki gave her and his photo. The day Chami and Kazuaki had their last fight, Kazuaki removed the ring from Chami's hand and had been wearing the ring on his pinky finger when he died.

After Kazuaki's death, Chami didn't visit the cemetery. But a long while after his passing, Kazuaki's parents called her and asked her to visit the gravesite. She had met Kazuaki's parents when they got engaged, and they had been wondering about her. That was the first and only time she visited his grave. It was there that she told them about the engagement ring.

"'I'd like a keepsake,' I told them," said Chami. "I said there should have been an engagement ring on Kazuaki's pinky finger. It turned out they were wondering what this woman's ring was doing on his finger. Then they gave it to me. I've been wearing that ring on my necklace and carrying his photo around with me. Sometimes when I feel real low, I hold the ring in my hand and look at the photo. Then I feel better."

When they were in Miyakojima, Chami kept the photo under her pillow. That way, she could dream about him, she thought. In reality, he never appeared in her dreams.

❦

BACK IN MIYAKOJIMA again, Chami and the crew stayed at Kazuya's family's home. Kazuya's father was in the construction business and Kazuya helped once in a while. But most of his time was spent hanging out with Chami and her friends, living carefree.

Looking back on those days, Chami thinks Kazuya was living off of his parents. But back then, Chami didn't care at all about that. She just enjoyed being with him. She believed that they were meant to be together and that their romance was a miracle considering her pessimistic outlook on love. The word "marriage" began popping up in their conversations.

At the time, Koriki was in Tokyo; she didn't make that second trip back to Miyakojima. Kaori and Falcon were planning on returning to Tokyo, so that left Chami and Kazuya — with the promise of marriage — on the island. Chami was twenty-three years old.

But Chami eventually found out that Kazuya had a debt of three million yen waiting for him back in Tokyo. Living the easy life on Miyakojima was not going to put an end to his debt. Chami suggested that they return to Tokyo and find work to pay off his debt before they get married. Kazuya resisted. In the end, Chami dragged him back to Tokyo.

Chami and Kazuya settled in the apartment Chami was subletting while in Miyakojima. It was a small five-tatami-mat apartment. Kazuya resumed work as an asbestos remover, a job he was reluctant to go back to. Chami found part-time work at a clothing store.

Kazuya turned out to be quite self-centered. Perhaps he was spoiled, an only child. Kazuya didn't allow Chami to leave home before him and expected a home-cooked meal at the end of the day.

"I'm the loyal type," said Chami. "I made a lunchbox for Kazuya every day, saw him off, then left to go to work. After I came home from work, I cooked dinner, then picked him up at the station. We continued that for a while."

Chami wanted to work both day and night to pay off his debt as quickly as possible, but Kazuya wouldn't allow that. She had to find work that fit into a schedule acceptable to him and that meant she could only make 150,000 yen a month. As for Kazuya, he kept taking time off, and that cut into his salary of about 200,000 yen. Life was hard. Chami no longer could afford to go out drinking — her favorite activity. Her friends told her that she had changed. She simply wanted to pay off his debt — not in two years as initially planned, but in one.

"Money was involved, so we fought all the time," said Chami. "Kazuya's from the islands — he drinks a lot. He goes out, spends money ... I even cancelled his credit card, but he went out and got another one without telling me. Every day was like money, money, money."

A year after they returned to Tokyo, Chami became pregnant. She had decided that she was going to get married and have the baby. But this being her first pregnancy, Cham was anxious.

"I really didn't know what to do, to be honest," said Chami. "I was totally unstable emotionally. We had debts, no money, we didn't know what to do and we fought all the time. He had flings with other girls and that caused even bigger fights. He threw at me the ultimate line. 'You know what? Get an abortion! I can't put up with your shit anymore.' That's what he said.

"I wasn't exactly being clear about it either. I thought I had to get married, but a part of me thought, 'Can I really love this person?' I never said, 'I love you' to him. I liked him a lot and I was happy when he said he liked me, even the part of me that shared a past with Kazuaki, but I couldn't get into it. I don't know. I guess I was having a meltdown at the time."

That evening, Chami cried and cried. She got an abortion on her own. Kazuya, on the other hand, was unable to do anything on his own. The apartment they shared belonged to Chami. Despite her repeated requests that he leave, he couldn't even find a place to rent on his own, so Chami had to do it for him. She gave him some of her furniture as well.

That's about the time Chami and her buddies met the owner of a fruit factory. He told them stories of a fruit parlor he planned to open on Ishigaki Island, part of the Okinawa cluster. But before they could go to Okinawa, they'd have to do two weeks of training at his factory in Saitama Prefecture, which abuts Tokyo. Excited, Kaori and Falcon both quit their part-time jobs and joined Chami in Saitama to work at the factory.

"The factory was for sliced fruit, you know, the kind they sell at convenience stores," Chami said. "Every day, we chopped a ton of pineapples and oranges. It was really fun."

The girls were on cloud nine. Soon they would be in Okinawa, selling fruit! They moved to an apartment near the factory.

But the factory owner explained that the company was having some funding problems. Their two-week training stretched out to a month, then two months. Ishigaki faded into the distance.

Months stretched into each other until the three of them had worked at the factory in Saitama for a full year. In the end, the women weren't paid their final salary as the company teetered on the brink of financial collapse. And after a year of chopping fruit, they were becoming a little bored.

That was when they came across the offer to run a bar in Kabukicho. Chami decided without any hesitation on the Kabukicho launch. That was May 2006.

❁

A LITTLE over six months after opening the bar, business began to stabilize. Customers were almost all repeaters, popping in a few times a week. Chami had finally gotten over Kazuya and was in a good place mentally. Although they broke up, Chami had trouble forgetting about him while she was in Saitama. She even visited him whenever she found the time.

"I think he was lonely," said Chami. "Besides, I do a lot for him — cook his meals — I'm handy. Seems he didn't find a reason to have another girlfriend."

As for Kazuya, despite his thoughtless words to Chami regarding their baby, he had time to think things through. After a while, he approached Chami about holding a memorial service for the aborted fetus. They erected a tombstone for the baby in Koenji and had a priest perform a ritual. Chami and Kazuya's relationship dragged on like this, and Chami was getting a little tired of it.

"When we first opened this bar, we were meeting a lot," Chami said. "But you know, Kazuya was also abusive, punching and kicking. I put up with it, but shit, I get tired of it, too."

Chami is in a relationship with a married man now. He is also a father, but Chami loves being with him.

Chami always carried around Kazuaki's photo in her wallet, even while she dated Kazuya. She also hung his engagement ring from her necklace. One day, the family man asked her about it, and she told him about Kazuaki. He said to her, "That's so cheesy." Nobody's ever used the word "cheesy" to describe her relationship with Kazuaki. It blew her away.

"Out of all the things people say about Kazuaki, the one I hate the most is, 'Oooh are you alright?' Or, 'Yeah, I understand.' You know? I'm not alright, and, no, you don't understand! I hate being pitied. What do these people know, that's what I always thought. Even if there was someone who lost her boyfriend, the circumstances would still be different. If someone like that came up to me for advice, I'd say, 'I dunno.' 'Cuz I really don't know. But then I was never called cheesy, so that was a shocker. I thought that would piss me off. Some time ago, I got pitied and got pissed off and I jumped on the person. But this one was different, so unexpected. My eyes turned into little black dots, like, 'Huh?'"

The man said to a speechless Chami, "What do you want to do? I mean, whatever." Then he quickly dropped the discussion. But then several days later, he called her.

"We're going shopping."

He took her ring shopping and told her to remove the old one. He removed the ring from a mildly suspicious Chami and slipped on the new one.

"Next, we're going to a print club,"[1] he said. "Replace the old photo."

In Chami's wallet is the photo she took with the man, not the one of Kazuaki, she said, fingering her necklace.

"This is the ring he bought," Chami said. "One time, I was seen by a Qigong master who told me I should get rid of the necklace. He said it's not good for a living person to become too attached to a dead person, including the aborted baby. I removed the necklace but within less than three days I had a panic attack.

1 A popular brand of photo booth.

I couldn't do it. But then at the time, when he told me to replace the ring, I didn't feel too bad about it. I felt like he was gonna turn everything around for me. I was worried that I was gonna flip out later, but I've been okay. So far."

Chami is still going steady with this man. Because he's married, she tries to keep it fun and light without placing too much emphasis on the definition of their relationship. But is she happy?

"No. Lately, it's become a bit boring," said Chami. "I like him a bit too much. I think I've forgotten how to be in love. This is an illicit affair, so even if I get jealous, I can't let him know. He's sort of frivolous. His wife probably doesn't care all that much. But I bet they fight a lot more now that I'm a part of his life. My favorite line these days is, 'I just want a normal kind of relationship.' At this point, I'd be happy if I could meet someone who could mean more to me than Kazuaki. I'd like to get married, have kids. I'm still searching."

Chami says that her appearance belies her true nature. "It's become a habit for me to play tough so people may think I'm strong," said Chami. "But I cry a lot and I'm basically a weak person." She mentally blanks out and at times experiences panic attacks. But she loves her bar.

"Life is like a matsuri," Chami said. "It's a cycle — festive one moment, then all gone the next." At least, that's how she's moved through the events of her life, riding the momentum of one thing to arrive at the next. "Through hard and sad times, my gang's been here for me. That's why I can run at full speed."

Another long evening in Shinjuku is about to begin.

JOINT VENTURE

Emi Nagaya, Landowner, 42

IT'S ELEVEN-THIRTY on a crystal clear spring day. A grey S-Class Mercedes Benz stops in front of a preschool in the corner of a quiet residential section of Tokyo. A pair of fashionable pumps, followed by two long legs, extend from the driver's side. Emi emerges, her skirt and trench coat fluttering in the wind. She smiles and offers greetings as she wades through the crowd toward the classroom of her five-year-old daughter, who has just started school. Today, Emi is going to check out a preparatory school that will help her little daughter get ready for the primary school entrance exams. Emi's hair is curled just right, her nails are done, and her face is made up in a colorful but restrained way. She carries herself as if she were a celebrity.

She is often told that she "doesn't look like a mother." It's probably just flattery, but it doesn't feel bad, she must admit. She is not about to lose her sense of fashion and style just because she becomes a mother or turns forty. Refinement is not all vanity, Emi believes, but something you do to improve yourself.

For Emi, cars are also about style. Her family lives near the center of the city, with easy access to trains and the subway. She doesn't need a car, and it is an expensive way to travel around Tokyo, but she has loved to drive since her single days. Wherever she goes, including to and from her daughter's preschool, Emi drives. Her dad was an auto enthusiast, and he happily bought Emi and her two sisters top-of-the-line cars to drive. Emi inherited her Benz when her dad died two years ago, but she still remembers how he bought her a bright red Audi 80 when she got her driver's license at eighteen. From that point on, she drove in style — an Audi ninety, a Mercedes Benz 230, a Benz CLK 320 with a four-valve engine. She wouldn't say this to just anyone, but it was hard even to think of being like the mothers in the neighborhood, pumping the pedals of their bicycles, their kids strapped into the extra seat, the big daikon radish sticking out of the grocery bag in the front basket, the disheveled hair ...

Emi was shocked to find that some people found her stuck up. Sometimes friends would tell her, "I thought you were scary at first." Perhaps it was because she wasn't a very good communicator, but whatever the reason, she seemed to often be disconnected from conventional wisdom.

Emi's family — the Nagayas — were known in these parts as landowners, dating back to the Edo Period (1603–1867). The family had owned land for seventeen generations. For Emi's wedding, her father tore down a single house on almost 2,200 square meters of land and built a four-story apartment building. The daughters and their husbands and Emi's parents took up about one-quarter of the building for their living quarters, and the other three-quarters were rented out to tenants. "Once I've passed, you'll be alright," her dad would say. Because of his thoughtfulness, Emi and her husband never had to worry about paying the rent.

When her father died, the family had to dispose of some of the property and buildings, but their holdings were still considerable. Back in her father and grandfather's generations, however, there was nobody in the vicinity who was unaware of the Nagayas. They wielded plenty of economic influence. Thanks to them, Emi and her sisters could grow up on this spacious estate without a care in the world.

But there were times when her reputation as a landowner got bent out of proportion. The neighbors would whisper as the daughter went to school — "there goes the Nagaya girl" — and friends would often begrudgingly comment that Emi "had it easy because you're surrounded by rich people." Her mom used to tell her how she would show up at PTA meetings around the time that rent was due, and as she walked in the room, people who owed her rent would stop talking and scatter.

Emi was educated in a private school that ran from elementary school to junior college. She did all her schooling there, eventually emerging with a junior college degree. Emi never felt like the daughter of a famous landowning family when she was growing up. Perhaps that's because her school had many students from affluent families and it was a bit removed from Emi's neighborhood. Also, she was the youngest of three girls — a full nine years younger than her eldest sister and six years younger than the middle sister. While their father was strict with the two older girls, he had become something of a softy toward Emi.

Emi ended up going to a branch of her school for junior college, where she majored in child-care and received a certificate as a preschool teacher. But she didn't really have much of a career plan. Her school was known for educating young women and preparing them for marriage. It was a girls' school all the way from kindergarten to junior college. When Emi graduated from high school in the early eighties, the conventional thinking in her social circles was that a proper woman would quit her job when she got married and tend to her home.

In those days, a women's junior college featured courses like child care, housekeeping, fashion and maybe literature. Of course, she could have elected to apply to a full-fledged university, but most of her classmates continued on to the junior college, too. Many of the parents sending their daughters to junior college felt that sending them to a four-year college would decrease their marriage prospects, and the school itself didn't really support students in their bid to further their education. The most common path among her classmates was either to graduate with a teaching certificate, as Emi had, or a degree as a dietician. Emi chose her path because teaching seemed like a pretty good temporary job that might help her when she had her own children. But when she actually did some hands-on training in the classroom, she quickly realized it wasn't for her.

"If I became a teacher, I wouldn't be able to grow out my nails and I'd have to play with the kids, showing my underwear as I slid down the slide, wouldn't I? In the end, my desire to be fashionable came first; I knew that there was no way I could do this job."

❀

EMI REALLY didn't have any clear objective to pursue. As she was starting to wonder what she would do with her life, her father came to her with a job he had found through his personal connections: it would involve clerical work at a financial institution formerly part of the Mitsubishi group. Emi speculated that her father, who had never had close ties to the Mitsubishi empire, may be using her job to develop his own connections. She told her father that she frankly had no interest or knowledge in finance, but it sounded better than being a preschool teacher, so she took the job.

But this job was more than she could take. For one, at the morning meeting, the staff would have to stand in line and listen to the boss' speech. Emi's work consisted mostly of handling questions and claims about pay slips and the like over the phone. She was surprised to find that outside of her lunch hour she was only allowed one five-minute break in the morning and another in the afternoon. At any other time, if she wanted to get a drink of water or go to the toilet, she had to get permission from her boss. And when an employee made a mistake, he or she would be scolded by the bosses in front of everyone. For Emi, who had waltzed through school without a worry, corporate life was where she experienced her first embarrassments at the hands of people more powerful than her. A steady paycheck was alluring to most office ladies — get that bonus and buy a new Prada handbag — but it provided no incentive for Emi. She couldn't understand why anyone would continue to put up with this abusive treatment for such little pay. Emi lasted a little less than a year before quitting.

After that, Emi traveled overseas and helped her mother around the house for a while. But she tired of this, too, after almost another year had passed. She had no reason to wear make-up while helping mother around the house, and she had all these new clothes that she had bought but nowhere to wear them. Most of her friends were working, and it was hard to meet up with them. Then, even when she did go out with friends, she felt left out of all the work conversation.

"One day, when I saw my reflection in the mirror, I looked so ugly! I was turning into this blah of a person. I thought, 'Oh no. I have to go back to work.'"

Her next job was as a contract worker with a big computer company. As usual, she was assigned to support the administration and sales teams, but this company had a different atmosphere — it was energetic and people tried to help each other. Emi had finally found her place.

Later, her boss came to her and offered her a position in a new joint venture the company was forming. "I'm going to join it. Won't you, too?" Emi left to join the startup at the age of twenty-four. Why did her boss recruit her? "I figure he wanted me at the new office to brighten up the atmosphere. I supported everyone in the old company, so if I were coming, others would follow. I think he was able to see my value in an everyday work environment."

For example, an employee would oversleep and call the office. He'd talk to Emi, hoping his boss wouldn't need to find out the truth, and ask her to cover for him. It was easy to share these workplace confessions with Emi. Excuses coming from someone as truthful as Emi may not have always fooled the bosses, but at the very least, they pretended to buy her stories. "This company wasn't one to get into personal details as long as everyone did a good job at work. People helped each other — that was more important. That's why they wanted me at the new company: to smooth over human relations," she said.

The new company had fewer people, a younger atmosphere and more responsibility for everyone than the parent company. It would be an energetic place to work. The new company was even doing away with the old job titles. Instead of calling the division head *bucho* and the section chief *kacho*, they'd now be Tanaka-san and Fujimori-san. Emi liked this liberal approach. She was selected for a sales position that covered everything from PCs to enterprise-class machines. Emi still didn't think of herself as a career woman nor did she think that she was particularly suited for the competitive sales world. She wasn't particularly confident either, but when her boss took her aside and said, "I know you can do this," part of her started to believe that, yes, she could.

Things didn't all go smoothly at first. "I had spent all my grade school days in private girls' schools, so I look back and think that when I started, I was completely unprepared."

She'd go out on sales calls and have this feeling that she was always a few steps behind when it came to conventional wisdom and money sense. Her family had been in sales of sorts with their generations of real estate deals, but the traditional relationship between landowner and renter that she was familiar with sort of had a reverse effect on her job. She simply didn't understand the amount of persuasion that was needed to get people to buy a product.

Her first job was to make sales calls over the phone. She would make more than one hundred calls a day. She couldn't help but think that if someone were trying to sell her something over the phone, she would just hang up. It was difficult from that point to muster up the persuasion necessary to get people to buy her products. When she was sent out on sales calls that didn't go well, she felt horrible and broke down in tears at times. "I kept bumping up against a wall and thinking, 'I just can't do this,'" Emi recalls.

Emi knew that one of the thickest walls she would face was the one meant to keep women in their place. This was the early 1990s, and selling computer hardware was still very much a man's business. When she would make sales calls, she'd sometimes be greeted bluntly with, "Huh? They sent a woman?" and even worse, she had to deal with guys who would pretend to reach for something and let their hands graze her ass. Then there was the time she was sent to a far-off city to make a sales call. The man she met there told her, "You've come so far, at least let me take you out to dinner." She really couldn't say no to dinner with a client, but the night ended badly, with him insisting over and over that they go to a hotel together.

The term "*seku hara*,"[1] short for sexual harassment, started being widely used in Japan in the late 1980s. In the 1990s, however, women in sales jobs still were expected to use their sexuality and charm to their advantage, and sexual harassment was far from fading away. Emi's company had done a good job of eliminating sexual harassment from the office setting, but once she took one step out the door, it was very much a man's world.

When she was harassed by a client, she didn't want to tell him off bluntly, so she'd escape with a joke if she could. In the beginning, when her wit didn't get her out of these jams, it would often come back to hurt her. She knew she was doing the right thing when she warded off their advances with jokes, but as a general rule, this didn't fly with customers. It was a rule that caused her pain. On the other hand, because she was young and female, she'd sometimes run into a customer who would treat her like his daughter. Perhaps they took pity on this twenty-something woman working in a man's world. Whatever the reason, her sales began to climb.

As the company grew, Emi's position within it also grew. This was a booming time for Japan, in the midst of an economic bubble, and the company's results were shooting straight up like an enthusiastic student raising her hand. At the same time, Emi's talent was becoming more and more apparent.

1 セクハラ. In 1989, a former employee of a publishing company filed suit against her former boss and company, creating Japan's first legal case of sexual harassment.

But Emi was humble. "In those days, my sales were coming from people who liked me and believed in me. It wasn't because I was a good salesperson, it was because they liked me. That was OK, but when one of my fans was transferred, the sales would dry up. I knew I had to improve my sales abilities."

EMI THREW herself into her job in part because there were changes at home. Emi, the baby of three sisters, didn't really feel connected to the family problems that were surfacing. Everyone was waiting for the eldest sister to get married and bring a son-in-law into the family, but she never seemed to be able to find a man who would agree to become a Nagaya.[1] Meanwhile, the middle daughter got married and left the house. By the time the eldest sister had found a boyfriend, she was thirty.

It was true that the Japanese were getting married later and later. In 2004, the average age for a first marriage was 29.6 for men and 27.8 for women, but the trend toward marrying late was even more pronounced in the cities. In Tokyo, the average age for a first marriage was 30.5 for men and 29.4 for women, according to statistics gathered by the Ministry of Health, Labor and Welfare. For a woman to be thirty and single, then, was quite common. However, in those days, it was said that a woman who was still single at age twenty-five was like a Christmas cake that hadn't been sold by Christmas. The single women over twenty-five — the unsold Christmas cakes — were often talked about behind their backs: "She's a leftover."

When Emi's eldest sister found a boyfriend, the family was hopeful that a wedding would soon follow. But when their fa-

1 It is still fairly common for men to marry into a woman's family in Japan, taking the wife's family name as his own, especially when family business concerns are involved.

ther talked to her boyfriend about joining the family and becoming an heir the young man would have none of it. Emi's mother pleaded with her husband to give up his plans of bringing in an heir for the family business. "If you don't let her get married this time, there may not be a next," she said, crying for her daughter. In the end, the father relented, and Emi's eldest sister was married.

On the night of the wedding, Emi's father's voice was shaking as he spoke to her: "This family has had sixteen generations of landowners. I cannot let the chain be broken by my generation. I'm asking you, please, continue the line." Emi had never seen her father look so weak, and she realized how important this was to him. Ever since her eldest sister had left the house to get married, father hadn't been himself. Emi started to feel that it was up to her to make this right. At the same time, Emi was still in her early twenties at this point. She figured rather casually that at some point she'd find a husband to join their family and run the business. It all remained very vague and unreal to her.

Emi had had a few boyfriends, but she was selfish, and if a relationship became unpleasant, she'd end it before long.

But a change came over Emi as she continued working. She started to realize how difficult business could be and began thinking that if she and her husband were to inherit the family business, she'd have to study up on it. She also watched as her friends got married and started dealing with the inevitable friction with their in-laws. Even if a man would agree to marry her and join her family, he may not want to run the family business, she began thinking. This could be difficult. Many couples get into trouble over family property or home loans, and her family's enormous wealth may even pose a hindrance to a happy married life, she worried. And if she died before him, the property would go to him. What if he remarried and he and his new wife ended up taking the family land? She understood that was a little farfetched, but the more she thought about all that could go wrong by bringing a husband into the family, the more she thought that she should just inherit everything and manage it herself. In a way, she thought, her current sales position was like training for taking over the family business.

❁

EMI MET her future husband, Soichiro, when she was thirty and becoming quite successful at work. He was a salesman with Emi's former company. He was three years younger than Emi and had a handsome face with an angular nose. He was into surfing. Soichiro was perfectly tall and lean, with a healthy tan and white teeth. He was refreshing to look at.

Soichiro was among several employees sent from the parent company for training. He was to be trained by Emi. These employees were eyed with disdain by the staff at the subsidiary. They were the "rebuilding team" sent by the parent company to help the subsidiary ride out a difficult business climate. The employees at the subsidiary were unhappy that the parent company was pulling out some of the founding members and replacing them with sales novices.

But once Emi began working with Soichiro, her contempt for him quickly dissipated. He had a talent that extended beyond work. A gregarious sort, Soichiro was always rounding up people to go out drinking after work or go golfing on the weekends, skiing in the winter and surfing and yachting in the summer. He had an innate talent for rallying people and team building.

At the office, he sat next to her and it wasn't long before they were having dinner together nearly every day. Pretty soon they were going on day trips together to play golf, and in time, they became lovers.

One thing Emi discovered about Soichiro was that he was quick to feel lonely and needed constant attention in and out of work. Emi didn't mind that — she thought it was cute. His dependency on Emi continued even after he was transferred back to the parent company. Around that time, Emi had decided to take over the family business and began studying hard to pass a state exam for a license that would allow her to buy and sell real estate. She began attending classes three times a week after work so that she could pass the exam in a year. Emi, who went through life without taking any entrance exams, had to work real hard for the first time in her life.

Emi and Soichiro had been together for six years at this point. While Soichiro said he was in love with Emi, whenever the word "marriage" came up, he become indecisive. Soichiro's father was a civil servant; he didn't have a business to hand over to his son. But he was reluctant to allow his first son to marry into the bride's family and take her last name. Emi was thirty-six and wanted to start a family. She knew she couldn't put off marriage for much longer. It was around this time — when Emi was busy with her studies and marriage had become a point of contention between her and Soichiro — that the "event" took place.

That day, Emi was at Soichiro's house. His phone rang and he answered it. He spoke a word or two on it and hung up. She noticed how curt he was on the phone.

"Who was it?" Emi asked.

"Just someone from work," Soichiro replied.

After a while, Soichiro got up and said, "I'm gonna go buy some cigarettes," and left the house. More than half an hour later, he still hadn't returned. Emi became a bit suspicious so she called him on the cellphone. No answer. She intuited right away that a woman was involved. She opened the drawer of his desk and found some pictures on the top of the pile. They were all shots taken at Waikiki Beach in Hawaii. The dates on the pictures showed that they were taken during the week Soichiro told Emi that he was going yachting with some friends. One woman appeared in a few of the shots. Emi had a sense that Soichiro was probably with this woman in the photo right this moment.

Soichiro eventually came home, looking as if nothing out of the ordinary was happening. Emi slammed the photos down onto a table.

"Don't you dare lie to me!" she said and slapped him in the face.

Soichiro, shocked, said, "What are you talking about?"

Emi felt no need to justify her anger. "Don't give me that bullshit!" she yelled. She kicked him as she made her way to his door, jumped into her car and sped home.

Emi was still on the road when Soichiro called her on the cellphone. He pled with her to come back. He had something to tell her. Emi made a U-turn and returned to his place.

"I'll break up with her," Soichiro said. "It wasn't serious. Don't break up with me."

Emi asked no questions — nothing about who she was, where they met or what she did. "I'll think about it," was all she said.

Emi would eventually find out about this woman, but from another source. The photos in Soichiro's desk were taken by Kinoshita, a colleague at work. She approached Kinoshita at work the following day.

"I wanted to ask you about So-chan,"[1] she said. "I heard you all went to Hawaii together."

Blood seemed to have left Kinoshita's face. But Emi continued, "I saw the pictures. Who's that girl in the photos?"

1 Soichiro's nickname. Friends and family often tack chan onto a shortened version of a name as an expression of endearment.

Kinoshita scratched his head and said, "Gee, I can't argue with you Nagaya-san. You're quite perceptive. I guess there's no point hiding it from you."

He told her Noriko Yamagishi was her name and that she was Soichiro's friend from middle school. They ran into each other at a bar that was run by a mutual friend from their school days. She was working there part-time.

Soichiro began frequenting the bar, Emi later found out, and before long, he was sleeping with Noriko. During their middle school days, Soichiro was athletic and friendly and had many admirers, Noriko being one of them.

Although Soichiro was single, everybody around him knew about Emi, so when he took Noriko on the Hawaii trip, he got hassled by his friends.

"I tried to stop him, too," Kinoshita said. "But he wouldn't listen. I felt bad about the whole thing because I was part of the group."

Emi didn't tell Soichiro a word about what she learned from Kinoshita. Many thoughts swirled around in her head. She wanted to have children, which meant it was time for her to consider marriage seriously. But Soichiro made it clear that he didn't want to marry into the family. If Soichiro were unwilling to get married, this may be the right time to break up with him, she thought, especially because he seemed to have another woman.

But when Emi tried to break up with him, Soichiro insisted he would end it with Noriko. "Please don't break up with me," he said.

"Well then, what about marriage?" Emi asked.

Soichiro dodged the question. As always, he never gave her a straight answer.

But when Emi said, "Well, then let's break up," Soichiro would say, "No, I don't want us to break up." This sort of exchange dragged on for months. Then Emi found out she was pregnant.

❁

IF SHE hadn't gotten pregnant, they probably wouldn't have gotten married, Emi said. The moment she told Soichiro about her pregnancy, he said without hesitation, "Let's get married." It was quite a turnaround from a man who resisted marriage for so long. Three months later, they held a reception and registered with the city.

Marriage, however, didn't make Soichiro's other women disappear. He spent his weekends surfing, leaving early in the morning and returning late. On more than a few occasions, he was unreachable by phone. Some days later when Emi was cleaning out the car, she found a receipt for a meal for two from McDonald's in the wastebasket. Another time she found a highway receipt for a destination that was in the opposite direction from the place Soichiro said he was going. She found these things highly suspicious, but she didn't confront him about it. She was in the middle of her first pregnancy and was afraid of becoming emotionally unstable if something unpleasant emerged.

The other thing was, Soichiro, an adept salesman, could talk himself out of just about anything. While there were days when he came home late, he always did come home, and he provided for them each month. "We've just gotten married," Emi thought. "I'm sure he's not thinking about ending our relationship."

Still, her insecurities mounted. Being pregnant didn't help. She would get teary-eyed often while pregnant. Sometimes she would start crying when Soichiro came home. "Seriously, I even thought to myself, 'Why am I crying so much!' Now I know it was because of my pregnancy, but at the time, I really didn't know what was going on. I was a mess."

As for Soichiro, he often spent his days at home sulking, most likely because he was annoyed by Emi's drastic change in temperament.

By then Emi was actively trying to find out more about Soichiro's infidelities. She checked his cellphone, wrote down the number with the most frequent correspondence and called it one day from her own cellphone while he was away.

"Hello?" said a woman's voice.

"Is my husband there?" Emi said.

"Oh, is this Emi-san?"

This was definitely Noriko Yamagishi. She must've expected this to happen one day. There was no trace of surprise in her voice.

Emi found out that Soichiro hadn't ended it with Noriko despite their marriage, and now that the newlyweds were soon to become parents, she was adamant about protecting her family from this woman.

But Noriko was not backing down. "I like Soichiro. My feelings for him will not change even if you are married."

"What are you talking about? I'm going to have his baby soon," Emi said. "You know, you're just being used by Soichiro."

"I know that. But Soichiro likes me too. Isn't that why he comes to see me?"

As Emi and Noriko got increasingly heated on the phone, Soichiro came home. Once he figured out who Emi was talking to, he took the phone out of her hand and yelled at Noriko, "What on earth are you doing? Leave my family alone." Then he hung up the phone. This unleashed all the anger and frustration Emi kept bottled up inside. She yelled at Soichiro, "If you're going to fool around, at least have the decency to keep it discreet. Clean out the trash, don't leave receipts lying around. As for phone calls, erase records of them before you come home."

❦

A FEW months later, Emi gave birth to a baby boy. A year later, she was pregnant with their second child. She quit work and focused on raising her son. Just as her stomach was swelling up with their second child, she received a call from Noriko. It had been more than two years since their first "conversation."

"Is this Emi-san? Long time no speak."

Emi had been busy the whole year raising their son and rarely gave Noriko much thought, although she was aware that Soichiro was still seeing her.

"What is it you want?" Emi asked.

"I hear you're pregnant with your second child," Noriko said. "But Soichiro told me he doesn't recall getting you pregnant. Are you sure you're not carrying someone else's child?"

"I don't have to take this from you," Emi said. "I don't have to answer such a ridiculous question from you."

Noriko was quiet for a moment, then she said, "I got pregnant, too. But Soichiro made me get an abortion. You don't have sexual relations with your husband, so isn't that strange? You're lying about having Soichiro's baby, aren't you? You conceived this baby somewhere else. So why do I have to get an abortion?"

Noriko was clearly losing it. But Emi was surprisingly calm. She pulled out her journal and told her what day her last period began and that four weeks later she found out she had become pregnant. She also told her what day she had sex with her husband. The second baby was planned, she explained, so she had written everything down in her journal. After she took a deep breath, she continued, "Of course, there's no truth to your claim that I'm having someone else's baby. I didn't think you'd make me say all this.

"Also, you may not know this," Emi continued. "But Soichiro is fooling around with women other than yourself. He's nice, but he's a smooth talker and popular with women." Not long ago, while Emi was checking Soichiro's phone to find out more about Noriko, she discovered multiple emails from other women. The emails read: "The other day was great," or "Can't wait for the next time we sleep together." They were all messages that made Emi shake her head and wonder why Soichiro was sleeping around with such vulgar types. After she found out that his infidelities encompassed a vast number of women, Emi basically gave up checking on his every move. It seemed futile.

Noriko didn't back down.

"I know he's popular with women and I know I'm not the only one," said Noriko. "I still like him."

Emi realized Noriko was not worth her time. She just didn't get it. Noriko was in love with Soichiro, so it didn't matter what anybody said about him. But Emi, as Soichiro's wife, was not about to let Noriko pick a fight with her again, so she told her, "I don't want to talk to you anymore, so please stop calling," and handed the phone over to Soichiro, who was watching TV in the living room. "It's from Noriko-san," she said.

That was January fourth. A usually busy Soichiro was relaxing at home. He took the phone and yelled, "Don't call again!"

Emi knows Soichiro is still in contact with Noriko even to this day. Noriko doesn't call him at their home, but sends letters to Soichiro at work. There was no way Emi would've found out had he left them at work. But Soichiro, for whatever reason and despite all her warnings, stuck the letters in his work bag and brought them home, where they were spotted by Emi's watchful eyes.

"I've worked for a long time, so I've seen many men like

that," said Emi. "I've taken male underlings out for drinks or for a night out on the town. We've talked a lot about relationships. Sometimes I think it's a given that men have affairs. It's a matter of pulling it off well or poorly. I have male friends who are fooling around even after they got married. Even now, I go out to lunch with my male friends and they tell me quite openly about their affairs. That's when I think, 'Well, why should my husband be an exception?' I only ask that it be done discreetly."

Two years after that phone call from Noriko, Soichiro was caught again. He told Emi that he was on his way to Osaka for business. He had never traveled to Osaka for business, she thought. And what company in this day and age would schedule an overnight trip to Osaka?

The plane ticket in Soichiro's bag was for Okinawa, where Noriko had moved. She found the ticket when she was putting his handkerchief in his bag. Emi wasn't going to keep this to herself. After the children went to sleep, she grabbed her gardening scissors, slapped Soichiro with the plane ticket and asked, "What's this about?"

"I didn't really intend to kill him," Emi said. "Kill him then get caught? How stupid is that? I wasn't especially excited. I used the scissors to show him that I was totally serious."

The threat of violence worked. Soichiro, who is normally mum, quickly opened up. "I have no time for rest even after I come home," he began saying. "The children are all over me, and you make a sour face that implies I don't help out enough with the kids. I wanted to get away from all that annoyance."

This was the first time Soichiro opened up to her like this.

Soichiro was always childlike, seeking companionship and approval. After the baby was born, Emi's attention turned toward the baby and completely away from her husband. Soichiro showed little interest in raising children. When his son was born, he wouldn't hold him, saying, "He cries when I hold him." When the weekend rolled around and she sought his help, Soichiro would either sleep in or go out and not return all day. This irritated Emi to no end.

Emi didn't want to deny him his say in the matter and even understood how he felt. But there was no way she was going to let him take this trip to Okinawa.

"Call her now in front of me and tell her you're not going," Emi said to Soichiro. He called Noriko and said, "My wife found out so I can't go." The trip to Okinawa was canceled, but she has kept the ticket as evidence of his infidelity, just in case.

NORIKO IS convenient for Soichiro. Given Noriko's personality, it might be better for him to maintain some sort of relationship with her rather than push her away, Emi said. She could become even more aggressive.

Where does Emi find this magnanimity? Surprisingly, she says it is because of her improved relationship with Soichiro. As the children have grown, he has become a better father, spending more time with the kids, taking them out on weekends to play putt-putt golf, playing catch with his son in the backyard. As for Emi, she has become less irritable and more stable emotionally.

"I've stopped making faces," said Emi, referring to the disapproving look she often showed Soichiro. "He's made such a big leap even by beginning to play with the children. Knowing him and his needy personality, once the children grow up and become independent, maybe we can go golfing together, then perhaps things will change again.

"Not so long ago, I asked him a question, knowing he may not answer because of all the stuff with Noriko. But I asked him anyway if he liked me. He didn't answer."

If Emi were asked the same question, she said she would say, "Yes," although she doesn't know how much she likes him.

"Other wives call their husbands 'germs.' Now I won't go that far. Except that we stick our single beds together for all four of us to sleep together and I could never imagine sleeping on his side of the bed. As for sex, sometimes he'll approach me when he wants it. I'll consent to that, but I would never initiate it. I don't want to contract some sort of disease. I'm always aware of the presence of other women in his life."

In the past, when Emi mentioned Noriko, Soichiro would talk about divorce. One time Emi said to him, "Look, if you want a divorce, just bring home the papers." Ever since, he's never mentioned it.

"Those women out there may be able to fill a void for him, but the truth is, if he leaves me, he'll never be able to live a better life than this."

Soichiro contributes a portion of his income — 150,000 yen a month — toward the household. That amount, according to Emi's calculations, is only about a quarter or even a fifth of his total monthly income. His contribution stays unchanged even when he gets a bonus. That means he is free to spend the rest on himself.

Soichiro has told Emi that he helps pay off his parents' home loan so he has little in terms of savings. But then she found out that he had purchased a condo without telling her. She became suspicious when they received a tax form for property-related income. When she asked her father about it before confronting Soichiro, he told her, "That's probably because he bought something. Go ahead and ask him." She asked him. "Yeah, it was something for tax reasons," was Soichiro's reply.

In reality, the Nagaya family cannot survive on his monthly

contributions; Emi is picking up his slack. Common sense dictates that Soichiro is well aware of that, but he has not once mentioned anything about it, not even, "Are we doing okay financially?" Emi has never broached the subject of finances with him, either. But there's one thing she does without telling her husband: she contributes the exact same amount to the household that Soichiro does. "If I put out more, I think that'll tip the power balance and give me too strong a voice in this partnership. It's just a matter of my own peace of mind. So I keep my contribution at the same level and try to work within those means."

Emi also pays for the children's kindergarten and cram school[1] tuition fees. Soichiro used to pay the fees in addition to the household budget, but after Emi's father died and rental fees began rolling in, without any warning, he stopped his payments. Although Emi was shocked by this, she didn't say anything about it to Soichiro.

"Of course with rental fees coming in, I was clearly making a bigger income," said Emi. "It wasn't as if I couldn't pay for the children's education. But the moment my father's inheritance money started coming in, he switched over and stopped paying for his own children's education. That made me sad. It raised questions about his integrity as a person. If he had said something like, 'I'm sorry, this is all I could afford,' I would've easily said, 'Don't worry, we can work it out.' But to stop paying without a word."

Emi has not taken any steps toward divorce, but she thinks it may be a good idea to do so in the future.

"If I die, the Nagaya family's property will become his. And

1 Cram schools, known as *juku* (塾), ready young students for entrance exams as early as kindergarten.

if he remarries, what'll happen to my children, my sisters? That's why I think I should divorce him when I reach a certain age. Although I'm not thinking about it specifically yet."

Currently, Emi and her mother manage several thousand *tsubo*[1] of Nagaya family real estate. Renters make payments through the bank, and she doesn't need to communicate with them regularly, but every time a contract is up, they have to renegotiate. In Japanese real estate, even someone like Emi, who is past forty, is seen as a spring chicken. Older clients say, "Why do I have to pay this much money to a little girl like you?" She is always on her toes in this business, where being young and a woman can be synonymous with being unskilled. "Unlike corporate relationships, this business requires an emotional and personal connection with the clients to succeed, and yet we have to know when to say, 'Business is business.' It's very draining."

Emi has learned that the business has to be profitable enough to be able to cover the various expenses — taxes of all sorts, including property tax, and maintenance fees. She is worried that she may have to sell off some of their property. The inheritance tax on property in Japan is severe. Emi is wary of shrinking the amount of property her parents left for her.

She is faced with the possibility of looking after her older sisters in their old age as well. They've both left home, but the second one has divorced and the oldest is talking about it. Whatever their reason, if the two sisters return home, Emi will have to help provide for them. The oldest sister, especially, has no work experience. The rental fees alone will not suffice to help support the two sisters, Emi thinks.

Her mother left all business decisions to her husband, and

1 A tsubo (坪) is 3.3 square meters.

knows very little about the business. Her mother seems to be relieved that Emi, with her sales experience, has taken over the family business. But nobody — neither her older sister nor her mother — understands how difficult her work is.

Faced with the possibility of her older sister's return, Emi has launched a new company. The three sisters love fashion, clothes, little trinkets. Emi thought that a store that sells imported goods and clothes might be a good way to secure income in the future. The business is still in its early planning stages.

From April, Emi's eldest son began attending a private elementary school. He spent the whole year attending cram school to pass the entrance exam. Her daughter will begin attending cram school for elementary school entrance exams.

"I didn't finish a four-year university, so I feel like I'd be more confident had I studied more. That's why I want my children to go to university. My son is going to take over this business, so I want him to have a certain amount of education under his belt. I went to a private school, so what my parents did for me, I'd like to do for my children. But then, I'm not the type to stay quietly at home. I think my sights are currently too focused on my children."

Lately, Emi goes to a fitness club with other mothers to decompress. She doesn't dislike drinking, so every few months, she goes out at night with her friends. "I let off steam regularly, so I don't get that stressed out. I enjoy hanging out with the other mothers."

"The future is unpredictable; enjoy what you have now." That was her father's favorite line. He said it habitually. "One must find one's own path in life, regardless of what others say." That's also something Emi's father taught her. She thought Soichiro was that type of person, too. But "men change when they get married, don't they?" Emi said. "Outside of the house, he is so gregarious and sociable, then when he gets home he shuts up like a clam. I guess I've changed after I got married, too. That makes us even."

Emi's posture is perfect as the spring breeze ruffles her carefully curled hair. She put her hand on the car door, turns back, smiles and offers a polite bow before driving off in her car. ❂

RED CIRCLES

Misa Kobori, Housewife, 36

MISA'S DAY begins at five in the morning when she draws a bath for her husband, Naoki. She makes sure that the bath temperature is just right when he wakes up. She also puts out clean underwear, socks, a shirt, a necktie and a suit for him. She selects a pair of shoes that match his suit, polishes them and leaves them by the front door. This is her morning ritual; she has been doing it every day for almost a decade.

Misa remembers watching as a child as her mother helped her father with his necktie. She believes that it's her duty as a housewife to help her husband get ready for work even though friends tell her that no housewife does that anymore. "Aren't you spoiling him?" her friends ask. Maybe, but why change now, after nearly ten years of marriage?

Misa has two children — a nine-year-old and a six-year-old. The older daughter is in a K-twelve school that is connected to a state university. Misa didn't really plan it this way. She has always been skeptical of some of the extreme measures taken to get young children into good schools. While some mothers talked about sending their eighteen-month-old children to prep schools so they can do well on kindergarten entrance exams, Misa's eldest daughter was getting dirty in parks, being wild, playing.

Misa remembers applying for the school in a light-hearted sort of way. She learned that the mothers who hung out at her local park with their children were applying to this one school, so she thought to herself, "Well, why not?" The school was popular and only accepted a few students. In the initial screening process, applications were randomly selected, so for Misa it was like buying a lottery ticket — a winning lottery ticket, that is. The Koboris were the only family in the neighborhood to make it into the initial selection, and that drew jealous comments from the mothers whose children didn't make the cut. "You got lucky with the initial selection, but you can't rely on luck for the interview," one of them said to her.

Naoki seemed confident about the interview, saying, "She's smart like me, so she might actually make it." But Misa thought her daughter was ill prepared for any entrance exam. To complicate matters, the week before the interview, Misa, who was pregnant with their second child, had to be hospitalized because of a potential miscarriage. Naoki had to accompany his daughter to the exam. The daughter, who tended to cling to her mother, was calm, seemingly resigned to circumstances beyond her control. She carried herself in a relaxed manner, fearing nothing. When the good news came, Naoki appeared prouder than Misa.

The daughter, now in fourth grade, loves school and says she wants to stay right where she is through middle school. Misa is proud of her. But their second daughter was a different story. Twice, for kindergarten and grade school, they sent in applications for the school, with no success. She took entrance exams for several other private schools, but those attempts also failed. The second daughter was born with a weak heart and had to undergo surgery at the age of two. Naoki took pity on her and told Misa not to push their fragile daughter too hard, but Misa thought otherwise. She wanted to take care of her daughter's education issues now so that she wouldn't have to go through examination hell later.

Nonetheless, now that the option of sending her to a private school is gone, Misa has come to feel that a local public school may not be such a bad idea. Her experience with the local community has been positive so far. She has become friends with the mothers and established a sort of solidarity with them. Misa knows that she can depend on any of them if something happens. Sometimes she finds her kindergarten-centric life stifling, but she has learned to get along with everyone while maintaining a comfortable distance. Once her youngest begins grade school, she will have a little more time to herself — something she looks forward to.

Her husband is two years her senior and works in the sales department of a securities company. Like many other Japanese couples, Misa calls her husband "Papa" and Naoki calls her "Mama." Once a year, they take a family trip to a resort in Hawaii or Guam. They also take a trip to a hot springs resort with Naoki's mother, Kazue. At first Misa was somewhat uncomfortable with the presence of her mother-in-law during these trips, but she has learned to deal with Kazue from a comfortable distance. The children love Papa and he loves spoiling them. The three-bedroom condo Naoki's company has helped lease is not extravagant, but it is big enough and near the train station and the girls' schools. They live a comfortable life with no financial worries.

Misa is from Miyagi Prefecture. Her father left the corporate world to run a convenience store. Her older sister, Sae, never married and still lives at home. She used to work at a car dealership, but now she helps around the house and leads a relatively easy life. Every so often, when the urge strikes, she wanders off to Tokyo. Misa talks to Sae a few times a week on the phone. They don't talk about anything specific but sometimes they end up chatting for hours. Misa takes a long break during summer and winter vacation to go back to her parents' home with the children. At her parents' place, her mother and sister take care of her children so Misa can go out drinking with friends and go to the beauty salon. It's like being on holiday, though a modest one. To be honest, it hasn't been easy being far away from home, raising the children by herself while Naoki puts in long hours at work. When she doesn't feel well, she pines for the comfort of home. There were times when she felt envious of friends who had parents living nearby. Partly because of that, she felt entitled to enjoy herself a little whenever she returned home to her parents' place.

Misa arrived in Tokyo eighteen years ago. It took her awhile to overcome a dislike for Tokyo that Sae had helped instill. Her mother's hometown was Saitama Prefecture, which neighbors Tokyo, and Sae made frequent trips to the capital. But when it came time to decide on a school, Sae said, "Tokyo is great for having fun, but I don't want to live there. The air is unclean and the water tastes horrible." She enrolled in a school closer to home. "When you walk around Tokyo, the insides of your nose turn black and your nose hairs grow longer," Sae used to say. That must have rubbed off a little on Misa, who thought, without much conviction, that she would go to a local university also.

It was around then that a relative recommended a university in Tokyo where he worked. She took an exam for the Buddhism department and got accepted. Misa was not really an ardent student of Buddhism, but she was surrounded by relatives who were in one way or another connected with a temple. She was also vaguely attracted to the notion of majoring in something unique. Her father, having lived in Tokyo during his youth, encouraged her to continue her studies there. Her interest in Tokyo began to grow.

Misa believed that each destination of her life was determined by her connections, not arrived at by some strong conviction on her part. She felt that the choices she made were not necessarily made by her but for her, as if someone had gently pushed her from behind and there she was, all settled in.

❦

WHEN MISA was a senior at university, she considered becoming a nun. After all, she had spent the last few years of her higher education concentrating on Buddhist studies. But to go into training, she would have to shave off her long hair. That was one thing she was never going to do.

As she contemplated her future, she was referred by a relative to a bank that had just completed a merger, and before she knew it, she was working there. Misa left her aunt's house and began living alone in the city. At the bank, she worked as a teller and processed a lot of paperwork. The work was busy, but the days rolled by relatively peacefully.

It was winter during her first year at the bank and Misa was twenty-three when she met Akira. Misa and some colleagues went to a bar in Roppongi that was frequented by foreigners. It was a trendy spot at the time. Her friends talked her into going, she says, and when they arrived, they realized they were very overdressed for this casual bar. They had come from a French restaurant and were still in their business attire, but everybody in the bar wore jeans or other rough attire. Smokers threw their butts on the ground. As soon as she walked in and had a look around, she thought, "I don't like this. I want to go home." But her friends darted deep into the bar. She settled down at the counter and managed to order a drink for herself, feeling awkward.

Right then, a man asked her, "What's wrong? Are you bored?"

"No, I'm not dressed properly for this place," Misa mumbled.

Akira was tall and fresh-faced — Misa's type. But she was uncomfortable at this bar. Roppongi was known for its pickup joints, and being hit on in one of these bars was not Misa's idea of romance. Their conversation soon petered out.

Eventually, her friends came back and they began talking about leaving. As they were ready to leave, Akira turned to her: "I can take you home."

"Sorry. I've gotta go. Bye."

"Can I have your phone number?"

Misa blurted out a fake number.

"What? What was the number again?" Akira asked.

Misa was caught off guard. She couldn't remember the fake number, so she ended up giving him her real number.

Akira didn't have anything to write on, so he kept asking her to repeat it. She relented and repeated her real phone number several times. That evening, he called her.

AKIRA WAS two years younger than Misa. He studied at a university in the US but returned to Japan without completing his studies. He took up a part-time job in Tokyo and has stayed there since. Akira was kind and fun to be with. Perhaps because she was a little older than him, he took her opinions seriously. Mostly, she enjoyed his friendship. When it came time to talk about the future, however, Akira had practically no vision. Akira's father was an entrepreneur with a hand in a wide variety of businesses. Akira himself was not interested in sponging off of his parents, so he didn't want to help out his father's business. She asked him, "Well then, what do you want to do?" His response was, "I just want to live life like a nomad. If I had to work, I'd run either a bar or a cafe, I guess."

"What you want to do with your life is up to you, but if you're serious about doing something, shouldn't you be preparing for that now?" To her, Akira was too much of a dreamer. Misa felt anxious about being in a relationship that held no promising future, especially after watching many of her friends get married. A part of her, however, felt empowered by the situation. She felt as if she had to stand on her two feet for both of them. After many frank conversations, Akira decided to go back to school and graduate. With Akira back in the US, Misa was in Tokyo by herself. It felt lonely, but she preferred that to his goofing around, particularly if marriage was somewhere in the picture.

Misa met her future husband Naoki around this time. She met him one day when her cousin took pity on lonely Misa and invited her for drinks with a group of friends. The group got along well and met regularly. Misa's apartment was in the middle of Tokyo, so many a drunken friend who missed the last train home used Misa's place to sleep until the morning. Naoki was one of these overnight guests. He was there as part of the group, though, and never alone with Misa.

One day, without any warning, Naoki showed up at Misa's place with a suitcase. Seeing the hesitation on Misa's face, all Naoki said was, "Oh come on. Let me stay."

"What? No, you can't do that," Misa replied.

But Naoki was persistent, and Misa finally gave in. Ever since then, Naoki spent most of the week at Misa's place.

"He worked in the city, but the company's apartment was in Saitama Prefecture," Misa recalled. "I believe he began coming to my place because I was simply closer to his office."

Naoki knew all about Misa's boyfriend in the US, but it was just a matter of time before Naoki and Misa became more than roommates. Misa said they went out drinking one night, then one thing led to another.

Soon after they began going out, Naoki asked Misa to break up with Akira. Naoki promised Misa he would "make her happy." Although Misa wasn't ready to dump Akira for Naoki, the proposition was flattering.

"I know this sounds petty," Misa said. "But I was comparing the two. Akira was still a student, so if we were really splurging, we would go to a family restaurant. We often ate at home to save money. Naoki, on the other hand, took me to the top floor of the Hyatt Hotel. We drank cocktails as we watched the Tokyo city lights glowing before us. That was such a strong pull for me. I've gone out drinking at such places with other older men from work, but this was something new and fresh to me. The romance, with the sparkling city lights in the background, had my head spinning. At the time, my friends were all getting married. I began to think that I wanted to get married, too. So I weighed one against the other: A man with an uncertain future against a gainfully employed Naoki."

Time passed and Akira was still unaware of Naoki's presence. Akira even returned to Japan a few times during this period. Misa would send Naoki home to his company apartment during those times. Akira never seemed to notice that Misa was living with another man. Whenever Akira went back to the US, Naoki returned to Misa's place. One day, an impatient Naoki asked Misa to break up with Akira.

"Well, I can't do that," Misa said. "You knew I had a boyfriend from the start." Misa didn't dislike Naoki; she simply couldn't break up with Akira.

It was around then that Misa discovered she was pregnant. When she had gone to the US in September to see Akira, they had had unprotected sex. She tested positive in a pregnancy test she took after returning in October, but she never told Akira about it. She only asked him, "What if I got pregnant?"

"You can do whatever you want," Akira said.

"I wasn't sure how to take that," Misa later recalled. "Did he want me to have an abortion but couldn't say it? Or did he want to start a family, but felt that he couldn't push it on me? The way I saw it, Akira had no income or position and to bear this child meant that he had to return to Japan, work in a job he didn't want and basically crush his future. That's why I thought I had to make a grownup decision."

Misa confronted Akira: "You really mean I can do whatever I want if I get pregnant?" Unaware that Misa was indeed pregnant, Akira said, "Sure."

Naoki on the other hand, was told about the pregnancy and that it was Akira's child. She wasn't expecting any response from Naoki. She just wanted someone to talk to. So she was surprised when Naoki said, "Okay, have the baby, and we'll raise it like our own."

Misa felt more surprise than joy at Naoki's response. Misa

said, "But things don't work out that way in the real world. Even if I did marry you, wouldn't you find this child a burden if we had our own child together? This is not like marrying someone who already has a child. Wouldn't it bother you to have to watch this baby that doesn't belong to you grow inside me? Your plan just doesn't make sense. I have my own ideas about this." With that, she dismissed his proposition.

But it was through this incident that Naoki's feelings toward Misa became stronger. Misa said Naoki may have mistakenly seen himself as the knight in shining armor, coming to rescue this luckless maiden. "I think Papa felt sorry for me. He said to me one time, 'You have no luck with men, I'll protect you for the rest of your life.'"

Misa still had trouble reaching a decision and continued seeing Akira. Two months after Misa had an abortion, she welcomed home Akira, who was back for the Christmas holidays, like nothing had happened. Naoki insisted that Misa break up with Akira during this time, but she couldn't bring herself to do it. She was no longer sure whom she really liked, and she simply stopped caring. As a result, she also began sleeping with Akira.

After Akira left for the US, Naoki asked Misa, "How did it go?"

But she didn't respond. Deep inside, she wished they would both go away.

IT WASN'T until late April when Misa discovered that she was pregnant again and events took a dramatic turn. "This time, it was Papa's child. I think," Misa said. She said she was ninety percent sure, but to be honest, even today, nine years after the fact, Misa is not completely sure that her daughter is Naoki's child. Misa doesn't know her daughter's blood type. She said she's scared to find out, just in case it reveals something she's not prepared to face. Fortunately, her daughter looks a lot like her aunt and everybody talks about how much she looks like Sae, which is pretty much where any discussion about family resemblance ends. The daughter does look like her father, but what if ... ? Misa tries not to think about that — it scares her too much. One thing for sure is that Naoki will never be told the full version of the story.

When Naoki learned about Misa's pregnancy, he said breezily, "Okay then, let's get married. I'll take care of you and the baby." Misa thought they were bound to get married, even before the baby came along. Her pregnancy merely pointed them in the right direction. At least this time, there was no hesitation.

When they decided to get married, Misa called Akira and broke up with him. She didn't tell him about the baby she aborted and the fact that she had become pregnant for the second time. She didn't tell him that she was getting married to Naoki. She doesn't deny that she lacked the courage to tell him. At the same time, Misa saw no point in revealing all this to Akira. In fact, it served him better not to know, she thought. Akira kept calling back, unable and unwilling to break up. Around that time, Misa had to be hospitalized from severe morning sickness, and after she left the hospital, she moved into a different apartment. She didn't tell Akira her new location. Akira called Misa's parents' home to track her down, but Misa's mother, protecting her soon-to-be-wedded daughter, just told him that Misa was not well and was in the hospital.

After that, things moved along very smoothly. Misa resigned from the company, citing poor health. Fearing that a shotgun wedding wouldn't look good, the couple waited until Misa felt more stable and held a quiet family-only wedding in Hawaii. The couple held a reception at a first-class hotel in Tokyo after the baby's birth, and Naoki's boss served in the ceremonial position of matchmaker or go-between. When former colleagues asked her, "When did you have the baby?" Misa smiled, "The baby was born way ahead of schedule."

Whatever happened in the past was past. Misa was now happily married, receiving warm wishes from everyone around her. Only one person, Misa's sister Sae, was against the marriage. She had her reasons. Misa always introduced her boyfriends to Sae, so when her sister came to Tokyo, she introduced her to Naoki. But Naoki had a troublesome habit of kissing everybody around him when he got drunk and that included Misa's sister. Afterwards, Sae was livid.

"I don't care if he was drunk! Why do I have to get kissed by my sister's boyfriend? And why are you laughing?" Sae said to Misa.

Accustomed to Naoki's strange habit, Misa's response to his kissing frenzy was a disinterested, "Ah, he's at it again."

But Sae's reaction was the complete opposite. "That's unforgivable. I won't let that heel marry my sister!" Sae's anger was such that it even shut up Misa.

It was years later, however, that Misa found out the real reason behind Sae's objection to Naoki. While Misa was in the hospital battling morning sickness, Sae had a chance to have a heart-to-heart with Naoki. That's when Naoki said, "I don't trust Misa." Naoki told Sae that Misa had dated other men and that he basically didn't trust her.

Sae shot back, "Well, if you don't trust her, why are you marrying her? We can raise the child on our own. You don't have to worry about her."

But Naoki insisted that he would do the right thing because, after all, it was his baby.

Misa thinks Sae didn't tell her about this conversation out of compassion. But now Misa feels a little remorseful about having married someone who didn't trust her, all because her sister kept quiet.

At any rate, wedded life was off to a good start. Misa's first child was born when she was twenty-seven. Three years later, she had a second daughter. The couple planned the pregnancies to be three years apart. Naoki suggested that it might be easier for the eldest daughter's college entrance exam to coincide with the younger one's high school entrance exam. Naoki bought Misa roses every year on their wedding anniversary — one rose for each year of marriage.

"How many roses will it be this year?" he would ask. For Misa, this was the best gift of all. In the morning, she would send him off to work with a kiss and at night, the two cozied up in their king-size family bed with their two daughters. Naoki worked in sales and was often called upon to entertain his clients or go out with his colleagues. Once in a while, he came home past midnight, but Misa had accepted that as part of his job. The only thing she has asked of him was never to sleep elsewhere, always to come home, no matter how late. They both kept their ends of the promise, and Misa never complained even if he came home very late. After their second daughter was born, Misa's life became very child-centered, but the couple remained closer than the average couple with children, Misa thought.

Their picture-perfect life began to crumble like an avalanche one summer when their three-year-old decided to play with Papa's cellphone.

❀

"MOMMY, THIS came out when I pushed a button."

"Don't play around with Papa's cellphone," Misa said to her daughter as she tried to erase what had popped up onto the screen. Misa noticed that Naoki had received an email from a woman.

Misa and Naoki had discussed how much they hate it when others sneak a peak at their email, but she couldn't resist the temptation and opened up the message. It was from Yuko, a colleague from work.

Several months earlier, when Naoki was hospitalized for appendicitis, Yuko came to visit. She wasn't especially beautiful, but she was energetic and two years younger than Misa. After Naoki left the hospital, Naoki and Misa took her out to dinner with their children as a sign of the couple's appreciation. The children took to Yuko, who liked to surf, and at the dinner table they talked about possibly having Yuko teach the children how to surf. Yuko wore a warm smile the entire evening. Misa said to Naoki at the end of the evening, "She's such a nice person." She didn't even consider the possibility of something brewing between Naoki and Yuko.

When Misa saw the email on Naoki's phone, she wondered about it for only a moment and concluded that it was most likely work-related.

Several days later, the younger daughter again brought Naoki's cellphone to her mother, Misa says.

"I told you not to play with the cellphone," Misa said to her daughter, who was at the height of naughtiness.

Misa took the phone and noticed this time that Naoki had sent a message to Yuko. Misa was a bit shaken by this. Why would Naoki send her an email? Misa sat with the cellphone in hand for an hour, telling herself, "Don't open it." But she couldn't resist and eventually opened up the message.

The message referred to a made-for-TV movie. "Let's watch that movie this Friday," her husband had written to Yuko.

Misa was planning to be back home at her parents' place with her daughters on Friday. Her suspicion mounted. Why would Naoki watch TV with Yuko while Misa was gone? "Perhaps there will be others from work," Misa told herself. "Naoki would never cheat on me."

Misa's trust in Naoki was backed by certain events in Naoki's life. Naoki's parents had divorced because of his father's infidelity; his mother raised him single-handedly. Seeing how difficult it was for his mother, Naoki used to say, "I felt sorry for her. I would never do that to my wife."

Misa had once said to Naoki in her mother-in-law's presence, "If I ever catch you cheating on me, I will divorce you." Misa felt a little insecure, but she didn't want to create a scene and hurt his feelings right before heading home. Misa told herself that it was probably some sort of misunderstanding and left for her parents' home.

❀

ON FRIDAY, when the movie was about to air, Misa picked up the phone and called home. He didn't answer. She tried his cell. Still no answer. She called him during and after the movie, but he never picked up.

The following day, Misa got in touch with Naoki.

"Did you see the movie last night?" Misa asked.

"Yeah, I did."

"Were you home last night?"

"Yeah, I was."

"I called you but you didn't answer."

"I might've fallen asleep. I didn't notice the phone ringing."

It went on for a while like that. Inside Misa's head, a thought was brewing, getting bigger and bigger: "He's having an affair; he's having an affair; HE'S HAVING AN AFFAIR!" But she didn't have the guts to come out and ask him.

Later, Naoki called her.

"I caught a cold," he said.

"Do you want me to come home?" Misa asked.

"You don't have to come home," Naoki said, adding that he

was planning on taking the day off from work.

A few days later, Naoki told Misa, "I'm going to the beach."

"You were sick enough to take a day off from work. Should you be going to the beach?"

"Yeah, but I'm going to be with a bunch of people from work," Naoki said.

"Well then, in case it gets chilly, make sure you take a long-sleeve shirt."

Naoki suddenly lost his patience. "Why would I take a long-sleeve shirt to the beach!?"

Taken aback by his outburst, Misa said, "Let me know where you're staying so that we can stay in touch just in case," and she hung up.

She never heard back from him and she didn't know where he stayed. His cellphone remained off. Misa was very suspicious, but she also believed that "cheating is not cheating until it's discovered." Everybody experiences moments of weakness. Even if Naoki cheated on her, Misa was prepared to let it go if he took care of it. Instead of making a scene out of it and turning him against her, Misa believed the best recourse was to let Naoki take matters into his own hands and find a resolution.

Misa returned to Tokyo as planned a month later, her emotions still in a state of disarray. Sae joined them for the drive.

Whenever Sae stayed the night with the Koboris, the entire family would go out to dinner, but this time, for some reason, Naoki didn't bring it up. Misa found that suspicious. After two days, Misa told Naoki that she had to return to Miyagi in two weeks for a doctor's appointment. That summer, Misa had had a mole removed from her face, and the appointment was to show the doctor the progress. This doctor was near her parents' place in Miyagi. That day, however, was when the whole family was scheduled to go see a Disney show; they had bought tickets for the event a long time ago. It was decided that Naoki would take the children. But when it came time to discuss who would take the extra ticket, Naoki suggested giving it to Yuko.

"We should ask Yuko to join us," said Naoki. "Remember the other day we all went out to dinner together and the kids liked her?"

He spoke of her as if nothing went on between them. Misa was on the verge of losing her patience. If Naoki were truly having an affair with Yuko, he had a lot of nerve to bring this woman to an outing with their children in his wife's absence. If he weren't having an affair with her, it was still an insensitive remark. Her anger surged.

That evening Naoki fell asleep with his cellphone in his hand. Misa removed the cellphone without waking him up. For two hours, she debated whether or not to check his email.

"If I read the email, I knew that I would have to check it regularly," Misa later recalled. "I didn't want to become that person and I also didn't want Papa to find out. On the other hand, I felt that I had to make things clear then and there, so I looked."

The evidence was clear. Several of the messages Naoki had sent to Yuko were proof of their intimacy. For instance, one recent email Naoki sent to Yuko read: "Why didn't you kiss me when we parted the other day? I don't care what people think." Misa forwarded each and every one of those emails to her own cellphone. She felt compelled to have them at hand as evidence just in case.

She was bothered less by the affair itself than what the affair said about his attitude toward her. "He thought I was a fool and he could get away with this," Misa said. Perhaps he even bragged to his colleagues that his wife lets him get away with things. Misa let him have his way and didn't complain about his late nights to create an easier work environment for him. This, to her, was a slap in the face in return for kindness.

That the woman he was having an affair with was a colleague, that she was only two years her junior, and, the fact that he openly talked about Yuko ... these were all unforgivable. "Personally, I think I could have forgiven him if he lusted after someone younger," Misa said. "If the girl had been ten or fifteen years younger, I think I would've understood. I would've hated it, but I would've understood. Why does it have to be a woman in her thirties? I think I could have tolerated it if she were in a certain type of business, if you know what I mean. This is a pride thing, I know, but I couldn't get over the fact that she was not a pro and was almost the same age as me."

Once she crossed that threshold, she could no longer stop herself. Without hesitation, she checked every single email. She tracked down Yuko's address, phone number and the day of their next date. Naoki sent Yuko a message saying, "I'll be there tomorrow so cook something delicious and wait for me." Misa and Sae planned to stake out Yuko's house the next day.

❀

MISA LEFT her two daughters with her aunt, explaining to her what was going on. Naoki finishes work at five-forty, but anticipating that he might leave a little early, the two sisters arrived at the station near Yuko's apartment by four. They bought a map at a nearby convenience store to confirm her address. "We need an energy booster for the stakeout," Sae said and bought Ripovitan D, a nutritional drink.

Misa and Sae waited in front of Yuko's place until thirty minutes past midnight, but the couple didn't show up. Maybe they dined elsewhere. When Misa returned home, Naoki was already there. She had told Naoki that they were all going over to her aunt's place, but Naoki was displeased at how late they came home. "They are still children, you shouldn't be coming home this late," he said.

Misa felt her blood boil. "How dare you. You were out with a woman," she thought to herself. But she calmed down and asked him, "Where were you?"

"I had to entertain in Otemachi."

Later that evening, she checked his wallet and found a receipt from a restaurant in Otemachi. Misa had no proof that he was with Yuko that evening.

The following day, Sae left for Miyagi. Misa was still distraught. Away from her family in Tokyo, Misa was left alone to deal with this problem. She had considered confronting Naoki. But Naoki is in sales; he was very good with words and she felt that he was going to be able to talk himself out of it. At the same time, it was becoming increasingly difficult for her to pretend as if she knew nothing at all. She decided to ask Naoki's mother Kazue to become a witness.

Misa contacted Kazue right away, but didn't tell her what the nature of the visit was. She kept it vague: "We just want to talk to you about our future plans. Can we come over tonight?" She told Naoki that she had to talk to his mother, and the whole family left for Kazue's house.

Sometime past midnight, after the children went to sleep, Misa said to Naoki in front of Kazue, "You're hiding something from me." Naoki's face began to twitch.

"If you can be honest with me right now, I will forgive you," Misa said.

"What are you talking about?" Naoki said.

"You're having an affair."

"What?"

"I said, you're having an affair."

For a while, Naoki bluffed but when he realized he had nowhere to run, he only said "yes" and looked down.

"Please write down on this sheet of paper when you two

dated, where you dined, what you guys ate and where you slept. And on days when you two had sex, circle the date in red," Misa said.

Misa wrote down all the days she was away from home and handed it over to Naoki. In front of his mother, Naoki was like an obedient sheep. He wrote down the places he went with Yuko, where they ate and where they spent the night. And, finally, he used a red pen to mark the days they had sex. Seeing so many days circled in red, Misa's temper rose. On the one hand, she wanted the whole truth, but on the other hand, a voice within her said, "Oh come on, I know you were doing it but do you really have to circle all those dates in red? Fib a little!" Misa felt like the protagonist in a poorly made melodrama where she transformed from the wronged woman into an evil force bent on retribution. The frightening thing was that she was kind of enjoying it. After Naoki wrote everything down, Misa said she had to go buy a cassette tape. "You come with me," she said to Naoki. "Otherwise you'll call her and try to make up a story."

After they returned, she turned to Naoki and said, "I'm going to tape this. You tell me everything that happened. When did you first meet?" Like a TV journalist, Misa made Naoki confess to just about everything — from the time that he met Yuko to their sexual relationship, and everything in between, including how many times they had sex.

Kazue was the first one to cry. Naoki respected his mother, who raised him by herself. He cared for her deeply. Even after he got married, he brought the children to his mother's place for birthday parties and stayed the night — that was a family tradition. Kazue was almost always invited to family outings, too. It was annoying to Misa at times, but Kazue loved her son so much that she was unafraid to say that she was proud of her perfect son Naoki. She even said to Misa that Naoki was unlike her husband and would never have an affair with someone else, that he would make Misa happy. So the shock Kazue felt that night was immense. Bawling, she prostrated herself in front of Misa and cried, "Please forgive me."

"Mother," Misa said. "Please raise your head. This is between Papa and myself. Forgiveness is a separate matter." Then Naoki threw himself to the floor and said, "I didn't think this was going to become this big of a problem. It's not a big deal at work. Everybody's doing it ..."

The apologies didn't really help. Misa was curious what Yuko would think of all this. It was already past three in the morning, but Misa turned to Naoki, "I'm going to her house right now. Please call her and tell her." When Misa was getting ready to go, Kazue said, "I'll go too."

Misa said to her mother-in-law that there were things she didn't want her to hear, but Kazue didn't listen. "No, I'm worried. I'm coming with you." The two of them drove to Yuko's house. In the car, Kazue said to Misa, "I want to know what kind of woman Naoki had an affair with." Obviously, Kazue felt some sort of anger toward Yuko, too.

In spite of the late hour, Yuko seemed to have been waiting for Misa. As soon as she let them both in, Yuko said, "I'm so sorry."

"When we had dinner together, you became friendly with my children," Misa said. "Why did you do such a thing, knowing that we were a family? It's one thing to hurt just me, but you were hurting my children, too."

"I didn't mean it to be this way," Yuko said.

"Then why fool around like that?"

"I wasn't fooling around."

"If we get divorced, you take care of my husband."

"Please, don't get a divorce."

This went on for a while. At one point, Kazue, sitting next to Misa, handed her a note that said, "Call her a witch woman." Misa found Kazue's interjections a little annoying, but felt a strong need to assert herself in the presence of her mother-in-law. However, Misa had become unhinged and her demands were soon spiraling toward the ridiculous. At one point, Misa ordered Yuko to call her mother so that Misa could talk to her.

"Please keep my mother out of this," Yuko pled with Misa, as she cried and apologized.

Yuko's tears were like fuel for Misa. She made Yuko dial the number.

Yuko's mother was calm on the phone. She listened for a while to what Misa had to say, then she said, "My daughter is not the only one at fault here. Your husband is partly to blame for this, you know. All sorts of things happen in a marriage. Life has peaks and valleys."

"I didn't call you to be lectured," Misa said.

"Then why did you call me?"

"Of course, my husband is partly responsible for what happened, but because of your daughter, our family is falling apart. That's all I wanted to tell you."

"I understand you're in a crisis right now," Yuko's mother continued. "But you can start over and rebuild — as many times as you want."

No matter what Misa said to Yuko's mother, she kept coming back with the same message: "It's tough, I know. Keep working at it."

Misa finally gave up, growing tired of the exchange. "Okay, I'm sorry for bothering you this late," she said and hung up the phone.

Misa wanted to smoke, so she asked Yuko whether she wanted to step outside. Misa also wanted the chance to have an honest chat with Yuko, away from Kazue.

"I'm sorry about calling your mother," said Misa. "My mother-in-law's presence made me feel like I had to be aggressive. I didn't really mean it to turn out this way. I just wanted to know the truth — why it happened and how."

It was during this time that Misa learned Yuko had been married for about six months before getting a divorce. Just when she was going through a difficult period, she started going out drinking with Naoki. At first, she didn't see him as a love interest as she knew Naoki was a family man. But Naoki became relentless in her pursuit of Yuko and she began falling for him.

"So you liked him," Misa said. "Papa can be quite aggressive."

Misa understood how Yuko felt. She had fallen under Naoki's spell many times in the past. Misa saw her younger self in Yuko, a lonely woman who couldn't resist the seduction. Suddenly, she realized Yuko was following in Misa's footsteps and felt sorry for her.

"I understand how you feel," Misa said. "If he weren't married and didn't have any children, this may have worked out. In a way, you were lucky I was the one you've had to deal with. Normally, you would have to face greater hostility from a wife with children."

Yuko began crying again. "I'm so sorry. I promise I won't have anything to do with him ever again," she said over and over.

Misa was saddened by the sight of this woman falling apart in front of her.

"I didn't come here to do this to you. Really, I'm sorry. But, it is your fault if our family falls apart," Misa said as she left.

❀

MISA COULDN'T sleep in their bed after that because Naoki had confessed that Yuko had spent one evening in it. He insisted that she only slept there, and they didn't have sex that night. At this point, however, no amount of apologies would diminish the memory of Yuko and Naoki sharing the bed. Misa has contacted Yuko twice since their meeting to discuss the bed issue.

"Did you have sex with my husband in my bed?" Misa asked Yuko on the phone without exchanging the typical pleasantries.

Yuko insisted that they didn't.

"Okay, I'll take your word for it. But how would you feel if a strange woman came into your house and slept in your bed?"

"I think I would not like that."

"Right. And I can't go into my own bed anymore. I'd like to clean the entire bedroom, so can you pay for that? I won't charge you for the whole thing. After all, it's something you did with Papa, so I'm charging him as well. You pay half."

"Okay," Yuko said.

Misa found that a room can be professionally cleaned for about fifteen thousand yen (about US$125). Half of that would be a paltry seven thousand yen or so — an amount so small it was almost embarrassing to ask for. The king-size bed, however, was a gift from Misa's mother. It was a luxury brand given to them as a family bed and a waste to simply throw out. She checked the company catalog and found that the bed had cost 800,000 yen. She called Yuko one more time to give her the brand name of the bed, the model number and the price.

"You can confirm the price in the company catalog. Half of it would be 400,000 yen," Misa told Yuko.

Misa had been warned by Sae not to tell Yuko to dish out

400,000 yen; that would constitute a threat, which could be charged as a criminal offense. Luckily, Yuko volunteered to pay, so Misa told her the account number and hung up.

A week later, the money was remitted to Misa's account. Misa never told Naoki about the money.

The bed has remained, but Misa has not slept in it since. Misa and her two daughters sleep in a futon in the girls' room, and Naoki sleeps alone in the gigantic bed. "Papa works late and leaves early, so we have to give him space for a good sleep," Misa told the daughters. The girls seem to understand. Misa and Naoki have gone completely sexless. The thought of having no sex with her husband makes Misa, a woman in her thirties, a little sad. But even imagining sex with Naoki feels impossible. She cannot say for certain that love no longer exists between the two of them. If anything, there is a greater love — a family love — that envelops the two daughters.

Misa has no plans to get a divorce. Not now, anyway. Her mother and sister both agree that Misa and Naoki have to help the older daughter finish school. Misa feels that it is their responsibility to keep the family together at least until the children can make their own life decisions. Privately, Misa feels that she needs to hang in there until their younger daughter finishes high school. Of course, if they can somehow repair their marriage before then, that would be wonderful. But that seems impossible at this point.

Misa notices so many happy families around her, and that makes her sad. "Why not me? What did I do wrong?" Some days she blames herself. Her life had been so focused on the children that she paid very little attention to her husband. Perhaps that was the problem. But when she reminds herself that she was the one who was cheated on, her pride prevents her from making amends.

On the surface, the couple appears to be getting on very well. Misa still wakes up early to help Naoki get ready, and regardless of how late Naoki comes home, if he's hungry, she'll prepare something for him to eat. Naoki is still kind to Misa. They lead a comfortable life and Naoki is an understanding husband who consents to just about anything Misa wants to do. Misa has recently joined a fitness club and on weekends she goes out drinking with her friends while Naoki watches the girls. Naoki may have an ulterior motive for his leniency, but as long as she's having fun, Misa can't complain. Marriage of convenience — that's what it's become, Misa thinks.

Recently, Misa had a talk with Naoki about their future together. For the first time, Naoki suggested a divorce. "I was the one who was cheated on," Misa responded. "Why do I have to be asked for a divorce?"

"Then what do you want?" Naoki asked.

"Like I've said, I want to try to make this work for the children. I want to focus on the girls."

"But if the parents don't get along, doesn't that have a negative effect on the children? I think separating is the way to go."

But when Misa listened closely, it sounded as if Naoki was concerned about finding a mate later in life. A later divorce would decrease his chances of getting remarried. "I don't want to be alone when I'm old," Naoki said. "If there's a time to separate, now is that time."

Misa thinks that perhaps Naoki has a girlfriend who wants to live with him and is pushing him for a divorce. Come to think of it, he's rarely home on weekends and he even spent last Christmas Eve entertaining clients. She's suspicious, but as of yet she has no proof of his infidelity.

The truth is, Misa has other reasons to be suspicious. A customer at her parents' store is an old psychic. The man is famous locally for his on-target predictions. Misa wasn't sure about this man, but decided to meet him anyway and invited him to her parents' house. Despite the fact that they met for the very first time, the seer asked Misa, "Did you have an abortion?"

"How did you know?" Misa asked.

"It's possessing your right shoulder. Do you sometimes have an uncontrollable sweet tooth?"

In retrospect, there were nights when, after everybody had gone to bed, she binged on sweets she had bought for the children. She thought it had to do with postnatal hormones, but according to this seer, the spirit of the aborted fetus was craving those sweets.

"You also seem to care a lot about this child, but you haven't even told the child's father about this, have you?" asked the psychic.

Misa was spooked by all this, especially because she had been feeling pain in her shoulders. She decided to go in for a spiritual cleansing. The ritual was simple. All she had to do was cut out a human form from paper and burn it. But no matter how many times the ritual was repeated, the right shoulder of the paper doll would never completely burn away.

"You must tell the child's father about the abortion," the seer finally said.

Five years had passed since the operation, but she learned through a friend that Akira had returned from the US, got certified as a chiropractor, got married and had his own practice in Tokyo. Misa wrote him a letter. She told him that she had had an abortion, that she didn't want the child to become a burden on Akira, who was still a student and so kept it a secret, that she had gotten married, had children and that for a variety of reasons, couldn't stay in touch with him. She hid nothing from him this time and apologized.

"I know it's been a long time since the abortion," Misa wrote. "I recently visited a seer who told me that the spirit of the fetus had possessed my right shoulder. He told me that I should tell you about the child and apologize. Please forgive me for keeping this a secret."

Later, Akira wrote back: "Thank you for telling me the whole truth. You've always complained about pain in your shoulder. I've opened a clinic. Please come in for a visit once.

"However, we are both married, so we shall meet only in the absence of romantic feelings."

Misa has been to the clinic a few times, getting treatments from Akira. The pain has gradually subsided.

Ever since then, she visits the psychic every so often. When he mentioned that Naoki was having an affair, saying this time it was a different woman, Misa believed him.

When Misa told Sae about it, her sister said, "Akira was a better fit for you. That's why I was so against your marrying Naoki."

But what's the point of discussing the past? Even if she married Akira instead, surely other problems would have surfaced. Misa thinks the important thing for her now is to live to the fullest the life she has been given with Naoki.

Divorce has crossed her mind as an option. In that case, she would have to return home to her parents' place and raise the children there. What would the girls think of that? One day, she asked her older daughter: "What would you do if Papa had to live in a foreign country on a long-term business assignment?"

Her daughter said, "Does that mean Papa won't return? Or will he return?"

"Hmm. Just what if he doesn't return?"

"No. I'd hate that."

The older daughter must have some vague idea that Misa

and Naoki are not on good terms. She might even feel like it's her job to keep the two together. The younger one also insisted that she didn't want Papa to go away. "I like Papa," she said.

When she considers the feelings of her daughters, she can't opt for a divorce. The younger daughter is only six, so there's twelve years before her graduation from high school. Misa must find a way to persist for those twelve years.

"Lately, I've been trying to look at the bright side of things," Misa said recently. "I'm quite happy in all other areas besides our marriage. I don't know if I'll want to share a gravesite with him, though."

Misa glanced at her watch. Dressed casually in her jeans and buttoned down shirt, this slight mother of two could easily pass for a young single woman. Her face without any makeup has a faint trace of innocence. But her eyes sparkled, full of a mother's strength, when she says, "It's time to pick up my daughter from kindergarten." ❖

ME, THE YIN YANG MASTER & THE TRIPLE-SHEEP

Reiko Suzuki, Translator, 42

SEPTEMBER ELEVENTH, 2001. The simultaneous terrorist attacks on America that left three thousand people dead are etched into our memories. On September twelfth, Japan time, the images of hijacked planes slamming into the World Trade Center towers and the subsequent collapse of those towers were repeated over and over and over.

On this day, I was at home watching TV. At the same moment in New York, many people were trapped underneath rubble, facing the end of their lives. These people did nothing wrong, and yet, in an instant, their lives were taken from them. There is no region in the human soul for the sadness and fear to go in the face of such illogical events. Before I knew it, I was crying.

But the truth is that this historic tragedy had come at a time when the stars were aligned against me. That was the real reason for my tears. That summer, I had been unemployed. I was stuck in a stagnant relationship. My daughter was causing trouble at school (the fact that it was minor trouble didn't make it easier). My child-rearing abilities as a single mother had been questioned by one of the teachers. I was approaching my forties. And to top it off, I had just had a job interview earlier in the day. My life was at a fateful turning point. It was like I was riding a rollercoaster—there was this anxious feeling behind everything I did.

I turned to a Yin Yang Master to help me figure all this out. He had given me one task to take care of that day: to put a period on that stagnant relationship. The master had divined my fortune from the date and place of my birth, then combined the fortune of my current lover and recalculated my future (this resulted in a very complex calculation). When he was finished, he presented me with four dates on which I could end the relationship.

"If you can't end the relationship on one of these days, your luck with men will most likely continue to spiral downward," he told me. "If you think about your future and your daughter's future, the best approach would be to remarry. But you only have a few years to do this. You need to quickly sever your ties to your current boyfriend and start looking for the next. The man you are with now is definitely not the man you were meant to be with."

"But he told me," I choked out between sobs, "that he is going to leave his wife ... and I should wait for him."

"I have explained this to you many times," the Yin Yang Master sighed. "If you don't sever these ties, you're dooming yourself to a bad fate well into the future. Listen, first of all, wasn't your reason for divorcing your former husband his string of affairs? You went to the trouble of divorcing him and cutting the ties with that part of your life, and now you're involved with a man who has a wife and children? How thoughtless."

I sobbed at his pointed reproach, but my tears were not from shame. I had no reply for him; his common-sense advice was right. It was obvious, I know, but I had no one else around me who would put it in such concise language. I had experienced the role of the "woman with the cheating husband" many times during this stage of my life, and yet here I was willing to put another woman through a similar experience. The contradiction was glaring. I asked him to leave his wife, and yet, that means discarding his family, and the children are trapped in the middle. I knew from my own experience just how difficult a situation this was. No matter how true I was to my own feelings, there is no way this sort of love should be forgiven. How long will I be able to say that my feelings were true? I knew from the start that this man was married, so I should have known that we were headed toward a painful sort of love. No matter how I said I wasn't lying to myself, somewhere in my heart, I must have been looking down on this man's wife. Wasn't I simply avenging myself for the pain I felt as my husband and these other women cheated on me? I may not have been aware of it, but that thought lurked in me somewhere. The more I thought about it, the more I found myself agreeing with the Yin Yang Master: my only path to happiness was to break it off with this man.

The Yin Yang Master had one more reason for deciding that my life with this man would consist of one difficult period after another. According to the master's calculations, this man was born in the year of the sheep, during the month of the sheep and on the very day of the sheep. In divination lore, people with a fate to shoulder are known as having a "special fate." It is very rare for a person to have the same three earthly branches in the sexagenary cycle, but sheep was the one sign I was not compatible with. It is the one sign where the stars offer no help. My affair with this triple-sheep was obviously an unlucky turn of fate.

"People with special fates may feel the tremendous grip of destiny, and the wrong partner may invite the worst to occur. Pairing up with this man is the same as gambling. If that's what you want to do, then fine. But you're already getting up there. Won't you want to settle down pretty soon?"

I hung my head. My nose was running. But I wrote the potential dates for the breakup in my notebook, even underlining them with a red pen.

Still, I couldn't make up my mind. I had done nothing on the three previous dates the master had selected. Today was the last chance for a "harmonious separation." And it was the worst day to do it from a human perspective. That's because my triple-sheep was from New York and his family still lived there. For all I knew, they could be entangled in this tragedy.

Rescuing survivors, providing repose to victims, working toward peace for all humanity ... At a moment when humans should be dedicated to these things, I was caught up in the fate of my love life. What a tiny, thoughtless existence. On top of this, I was desecrating myself and this man's family—he was another woman's husband. How many times had I cried over love like this? And yet I hadn't learned. Here I was, in another painful love affair, without a companion to mourn for me should I die. I called the triple-sheep to break off our affair.

"Is your family in New York alright?"

He was obviously shaken, but he had confirmed that his family was safe. I breathed a sigh of relief. If his family had been entangled in this, I wouldn't have been able to break off our relationship.

"I'm so upset," he said.

"I'm sorry to hear that."

"Thanks."

There was a long pause, and then I continued.

"Umm. Let's break up. The two of us."

"Huh? What are you talking about?"

"I said 'let's break up.'"

Silence.

He was at a loss for words. He was quiet for a time. Finally, he spoke: "Why do we have to have this talk today, now? Why does it have to be today? Are you that cold-blooded?"

I had no answer, so I hung up the phone.

A few minutes later, I received an email from him. It said, "I am very angry." When I think back on that time, I'm sure that I could have explained the circumstances to him, but how? "You are a triple-sheep and sheep is an unfavorable element for me, so it's useless to continue. Your fate consists of either great luck or great misfortune. But I'm looking to settle down. There's no way this will work." Would he understand what I was talking about? I decided to just walk away without explanation. I pressed the reply button and wrote "FUCK YOU" dozens of times, until the screen was filled with the words. Then, without hesitation, I hit the send button.

❁

I MET KAWAMOTO-SENSEI, the Yin Yang Master, through an acquaintance. Yumi was a single woman in her mid-thirties with a wonderful smile. She had worked for a well-known trading firm, but a few years earlier, she set out on her own. At the time, she was working as an interpreter and counselor. She was good at her work and her company began doing well, allowing her to buy a stylish condo in the city. To bystanders, she was in the bloom of her youth, but in those days, she was riddled with worries because she couldn't find a man to become her husband.

Yumi always had her hair curled just right and had a conservative but inspired sense of fashion. She seemed like the model counselor—calm and a good listener. Judging by her figure and her character, she should have been able to steal the heart of just about any man. Add the fact that she was successful at work, and it was hard to imagine a better candidate for a man looking for a bride. Perhaps because of all this, people would ridicule her: "She can't find a match because she's so fastidious. This guy's no good, that guy's no good." But the truth of the matter was that she had had horrible luck with men.

While still in her twenties, she wasn't able to marry a man she had spent years with. There were many reasons it didn't work. After that, she seemed fated to date only men she couldn't marry. Once she entered her thirties, marriage seemed very far off and her dates came to a halt. At this pace, she may never get married, she worried. Work was going well and she wasn't in need of money. But she wanted to have a child and be a mother. For this to happen, she needed to find a partner to marry.

I knew this about Yumi, so one day when she called on a work-related matter, I said casually, without thinking, "So, have you found a man yet?"

"Yes, thank you for asking. I'm getting married in four months."

"Wow, that's great. A sudden marriage! Where did you meet him?"

She hesitated before she replied. "Actually, it is all because of a certain Yin Yang Master."

"A what?"

Yumi kindly explained: "A person who understands the yin and yang in our lives. There are many interpretations, but there is yin and yang, and the power of the natural world—wood, fire, earth, metal, water—and directions. All these elements are combined to discern whether people's fates are compatible. Simply put, it's a form of fortune-telling. One faction of masters descends from the days of the Heian Court and preserves the art to this day. Most of them are well-connected to political VIPs, entertainers and financiers. The sensei I saw is much the same, but I was lucky enough to have the chance to learn from him."

Kawamoto-sensei told her that if she really wanted to get married, he would give her some homework to improve her fortune, Yumi explained. For example, he would tell her, "On the day of the rooster and the hour of the snake, collect water from the southeast." "Go to a temple in the direction of the rabbit, make an offering of rhododendrons, then walk around the temple grounds five times. Then pray three times and make an offering of seventeen five-yen coins." His directions were quite detailed.

Modern Japanese all know what year of the zodiac cycle they were born in and use it to understand their fortune and who they are compatible with. On the New Year, they send postcards with that year's zodiac sign, and they make a payment when they enter a critical year, known as a *yakudoshi*.[1] That's about the extent of their knowledge. Phrases like "the day of the rooster" or "the hour of the snake" are only used by Shinto officials, people who handle religious ceremonies, those involved in divination lore or some other sort of specialist. Most people have only seen the phrases in history books.

1 厄年. The critical years for men are twenty-five, forty-two and sixty-one; for women, they are nineteen, thirty-three and thirty-seven.

The sexagenary cycle dates back to ancient China. It is made up of sixty combinations from two cycles: the ten heavenly stems (yang wood, yin wood, yang fire, yin fire, yang earth, yin earth, yang metal, yin metal, yang water, yin water) and the twelve earthly branches (rat, ox/cow, tiger, rabbit, dragon, snake, horse, sheep, monkey, rooster, dog, boar). The practice is used in China, Japan and other parts of Asia to name years, months, times and directions.

Yin Yang masters who tell fortunes and conduct purification rites held positions as bureaucrats in the Japanese government during the Heian Era (794–1192) and enjoyed a firm position in society.

It was surprising to me that a modern young woman like Yumi, who had lived overseas for a long time and mainly worked as an interpreter, would devote herself to this ancient practice. But I also knew that she had an interest in spirituality, so perhaps this was a natural path for her. I recalled that when we first met, we had that interest in common.

One by one and with great sincerity, Yumi executed the tasks given to her by Kawamoto-sensei. His tasks included specific dates, times and directions, so there were several challenges for Yumi. But she said that whenever it looked like she was going to fail, some sort of coincidence would end up helping her complete the task. For example, when she had to gather water from a spring in a specific direction, she took a plane from Tokyo to Hokkaido in order to visit a certain spring and complete her task. However, when she got there, she found that the spring had dried up. The road was growing dark and the specified time to draw the water was fast approaching. All of a sudden, an old woman appeared on the road. Yumi asked without much expectation, "Is there a spring around here?"

"If you're looking for a spring, there's one right up there," she said, pointing Yumi in the right direction and giving her just enough time to meet the Yin Yang Master's deadline.

YUMI WENT to a lot of parties to meet her future husband, and she aggressively asked for introductions to potential suitors. In the first couple of months after having met Kawamoto-sensei, she started having all sorts of dates. Yumi would report to Kawamoto-sensei in detail about where and when the men were born, what date and time they met and what direction they were facing. Kawamoto-sensei would explain how her married life with each man would play out; he would draw up lists of their strong and weak points, ranking them as potential husbands. Kawamoto-sensei told Yumi to do the following:

» *When she goes on a date, she should state clearly to her date that she is looking for a husband.*
» *If a man proposes to her, she should not give a prompt reply. She should wait until at least several men have proposed.*
» *She should not have sex with any man until the time and date of the wedding has been set or she is officially engaged.*
» *A man who won't respect these conditions does not deserve to be considered as a marriage candidate.*

Yumi followed these conditions precisely, and within three months, three men had proposed to her.

"Actually, I thought I could get married to a man named Yamano, but Kawamoto-sensei did his calculations, and he came out as the lowest priority. When I think back, Yamano was sort of a dangerous guy and not the sort I should marry if I'm thinking sensibly about it, but for some reason, I'm drawn to those dangerous types. He was aggressive, and I thought that if we kept dating, we'd end up having sex. But he had a charm about him that made it hard for me to break it off. I had half resigned myself to just going for it with him. 'If it happens, so what?' I thought at the time. Then one day, a big rain came and I dropped my cellphone in a puddle. It wouldn't work. I had Yamano's cellphone number saved on my phone, but I couldn't access it. We had only traded cellphone numbers, so we had no way of contacting each other. I took the phone in for repairs, and it was fixed a few days later. Over that weekend, I was supposed to meet him, but I had no way of getting in touch with him. On that same weekend, Takasugi proposed to me. He's the man I'm engaged to."

Takasugi was someone Yumi knew from before; they were in the same social circle, and he had shown some casual interest in her in the past. But before she met Kawamoto-sensei, Yumi had thought of him as nothing more than an acquaintance. Soon after meeting the Yin Yang Master, she went to her group's monthly gathering and found that Takasugi was sitting next to her. After he had had a few drinks, he turned to her and said, "Yumi-chan, would you want to go have dinner some time?"

"I've heard that line so many times."

"Really?"

"Yes. But you've never asked me out properly, have you?"

Takasugi cocked his head to one side. "OK, then. How about next Saturday?"

That's how their first date came about. True to Kawamoto-sensei's orders, Yumi told Takasugi on that first night out: "I'm actually looking for the right man to marry."

He looked surprised but said only, "Oh, really?" Nothing more was said about it that evening.

Takasugi invited Yumi to many dinners after that. They didn't really talk about anything special when they met, but Takasugi listened to her, and she began to feel not a small attraction to him. As they continued to date without him popping the question, she couldn't decide whether Takasugi was too shy to ask her or whether he just wasn't interested. Kawamoto-sensei told her he was a good match. "You will be companions who can build on your good fortune together." But if Takasugi had no intention of marrying, there was nothing she could do. Takasugi was a good man, no doubt, but Yumi was still drawn to the wild side she saw in Yamano. Part of her thought, "It's only a fortune," and considered sleeping with Yamano. After all, he had said he wanted to marry her. When her cellphone fell into a puddle, Yumi had been struggling with this dilemma.

The dripping wet cellphone could be a sign, she thought as she faxed a message to Kawamoto-sensei: "I dropped my cellphone in a puddle and have no way of contacting Yamano-san." Kawamoto-sensei called her back right away. "You could be in for some good news, so in the morning, go buy some flowers and adorn the entryway. Then wait there, without going out, for the news to come."

She did exactly as he said. Eventually, the phone rang. It was Takasugi. "Sorry for not giving you more advance notice, but can you meet me today?"

That night, at dinner, Takasugi became the third man to propose to Yumi. Of the three, he was the steadiest and the best match for a marriage. "I never pictured him as my husband. On that day, if it hadn't rained and I hadn't dropped my cellphone, I'd probably be married to Yamano. They say things happen for a reason, but this outcome really feels inevitable."

IN JAPAN, there is a saying that goes, "It's still fortune-telling whether it hits or misses." Many Japanese turn to fortune-tellers at turning points in their lives. Japan's fortune-tellers are akin to counselors or therapists in the West. They hold a respected position in society. When people have worries, they first turn to a fortune-teller or perhaps to a Shinto purification ritual. If you say you are going to counseling, it sounds to the Japanese as if you have a mental problem. But if you're going to have your fortune told or a purification ceremony done, there is no social stigma attached. The Japanese tend to rely on others as they search for a solution. A sense of duty drives them, while issues of responsibility and cause remain vague. For a troubled person, it can be quite helpful to have someone to talk to as you face your problem.

In my case, it's not that I believe one hundred percent of what the fortune-tellers say. But I'd rather have a fortune-teller tell me "your fortune is bad" than hear from a therapist that "you have a problem with your past and your character." I know all too well about my failings without having a therapist point them out. To those who say I am teetering toward escapism, I say that I simply can't continue to bear this mental burden by myself.

After hearing Yumi's story, I didn't hesitate to ask her to introduce me to Kawamoto-sensei. But the sensei would have to decide on our compatibility first. He'd want to know the day Yumi and I met, the date of my birth, the location of my home—and he'd been known to turn down a request to meet based on this information. Still, Yumi said she would send an application to him right away. I hope it helps you, she said before hanging up the phone. The following day, she called me and told me that he had agreed to meet me. I called Kawamoto-sensei's office and set up an appointment for later in the week. A wave of relief washed over me because I had heard that it usually takes much longer to get an appointment and that many people never get the chance.

Contrary to my expectations, Kawamoto-sensei was dressed quite conventionally in a shirt and slacks—he was small and seemed like a tender man. But when he spoke, his words sliced through me. I felt overwhelmed in his presence. He told me that I was a domestic sort of person, even though I don't look the part (!), and I needed to have a harmonious base at home to be successful at work. There were a lot of reasons that I had married my ex-husband, but it was right to get a divorce. Now I should concentrate on getting remarried and repairing my life. As for my work status, he said I'll find work immediately, but I won't stay at the job long. However, don't worry about that, he said. Over the next few years, getting remarried should take priority over my career.

When I finally left the sensei's office, three hours had passed. Kawamoto-sensei charged thirty thousand yen (about US$250) for the first session. Other sessions would be scheduled as necessary. Compared with a typical fortune-teller's rate of three thousand to five thousand yen, this was expensive, but I had never had an experience where the fortune-teller seemed to get my situation so right from the very first meeting. He would offer advice via fax messages over the next several months, making the original payment quite reasonable

Kawamoto-sensei's first task for me was to sprinkle roasted salt around the perimeters of my house to purify it. My house is built on just about all of our land, and to get around it, a person has to squeeze her way through. Plus, the weeds were thriving. If I am going to purify the house, I might as well weed too, I thought. As I climbed out a window and stepped into a particularly hard-to-access area, the earth felt squishy beneath me. I yelped and looked down at my feet to find a black sheepskin rug that my ex-husband had brought from overseas many years ago. I must have been airing it out on the ledge, it fell, and I never thought of it again. It had been lying on the ground for years, soaking up rainwater and was now a soggy mess.

I felt a chill go up my spine at this frightening coincidence, finding this sheepskin carpet beneath the weeds ... I went back inside and sent a fax to Kawamoto-sensei asking him to explain the relationship between my triple-sheep and this carpet.

"When you give yourself over completely to the laws of nature, these coincidences happen at a faster rate. That carpet is something you no longer need. Thank it for its hard work, sprinkle roasted salt on it, and dispose of it."

After this incident, I pulled out an old journal of mine and tried to figure out the exact day I met the triple-sheep. Of course. It was on the day of the sheep.

After we met, I recalled having a recurring nightmare where I was surrounded by sheep and couldn't move. To rid myself of this misery, I redoubled my efforts to execute every task Kawamoto-sensei gave me. This was why I called the triple-sheep on 9/11—these coincidences kept piling up.

THIS TALE has a sequel. After the soaking cellphone incident, Takasugi and Yumi were married, Yumi gave birth to two children and the couple eventually divorced. For Yumi, marrying Takasugi was a step on the path to being a mother, so it was definitely not a waste. But she said that as she went through the divorce, she realized that she wasn't meant to live with a man—she was meant to follow her own path. For me, since I sent that "FUCK YOU" email and broke up with the triple-sheep, my life has taken many twists and turns, and I am now happily in love with him. I'm not sure what the future holds, but at the very least, I no longer have that sheep nightmare.

My path since I sent that email has hardly been smooth. I was sued for defamation by the triple-sheep's wife, and his attempt to get a divorce failed in court. Perhaps this legal trouble was part of Kawamoto-sensei's prophecy. It's difficult to say that his prophecy came off as expected, but unless you try something, you can't tell what is misfortune and what is happiness. I'm often asked if I've had enough of fortune-telling, but once in a while, out of mere curiosity, I knock on a fortune-teller's door. Mostly, I take in the convenient parts and block out the rest. It's still fortune-telling whether it hits or misses. The vagueness is what I like.

PURGATORY

Fumiko Yagi, Administrative Assistant, 40

THE STRONG OCEAN breeze that whips through the corridor between two high-rise condominiums hits Fumiko head on as she emerges from the subway. Usually, she can hide behind a throng of commuters coming home from work, but not tonight; it's already past eleven PM and barely a soul is in sight. The salty breeze ruffles Fumiko's hair and dances around her feet. Her cellphone, on silent mode, vibrates. She fumbles around in her coat pocket and, in a rush to answer the call, drops the cellphone down the stairs she has just climbed. She drags her tired feet, swollen from working overtime, down the stairs in small steps to retrieve the phone. As she reaches for it, the ringing stops.

Fumiko has lived here for two years now. She still dislikes the strong wind. Raised in the tony Yamanote area of Yokohama, Fumiko never imagined that one day she would live in a seaside residential development atop landfill. Fumiko's apartment building is small and old-fashioned, a fifteen-minute walk from the nearest station and very far in more ways than one from the condo she had in Jiyugaoka, Tokyo. She never considered her new living quarters an inconvenience, but she feels pained when she thinks about Yuna, her only daughter.

Fumiko attached a few conditions to her condo hunting. For one, the new home had to be within an hour's commute of Yuna's high school and Yuichi's place. Also, the rent must be no more than 120,000 yen (about one thousand dollars) just in case she would have to pay for the place herself someday. But most important of all to Fumiko was that there be a spare room for Yuna. Fumiko narrowed her search down to three places — this wasn't easy considering her small budget — and Yuna selected the one with a tiny balcony — just enough room for one person to stand — and a six-tatami-mat room she could call her own.

Yuna maintained a smile the entire time the two young movers were there. She happily served hot tea and chocolate snacks. The wind outside was cold, but Yuna wore the expression of a child at a picnic on a warm sunny day.

When the boxes were all moved in and the young men left, the two-bedroom apartment fell silent, and Yuna retired to her bedroom without a word. Fumiko spent about an hour organizing the kitchen when she noticed a box with the words "kettle, plates" written on it. She pulled out the kettle, mug and Yuna's favorite Fauchon brand tea and called out, "Yuna, do you want some tea?" There was no response.

"Yuna, are you asleep?"

Fumiko went to Yuna's room and found her sitting in a chair

with her cheeks resting on her hands, sobbing quietly. Outside, the setting sun spilled an orange glow of early spring into the south-facing window and onto Yuna's wet cheeks.

"I'm really sorry, Yuna." Fumiko put her hand on Yuna's shoulder to give her a hug, but Yuna flung it off and stepped out onto the balcony.

"You're so naive, mom," Yuna said, without looking back. "You grew up like a princess or something. You know so little about the world. There's no way this is going to work."

"Maybe I am a little naive and caused you a lot of pain, but I'm going to work very hard from now on."

Fumiko fought back the desire to embrace her daughter and instead gazed at her from behind, a silhouette against the late afternoon sun. She was overwhelmed by a rush of emotions: wonder at the fact that her daughter had grown so fast in just one year and repentance for dragging her young daughter into this predicament. Strangely, however, she felt no fear of the future.

❀

FUMIKO CALLED home on her cellphone.

"Mom? What? I was sleeping," replied Yuna.

"My cellphone rang and I thought it might be you," said Fumiko. "I just arrived at the station."

"How many times do I have to tell you this?" said Yuna. "Your cell number is already in the system. So is our home phone. You can tell who's calling if you look under incoming calls."

"You're right. I forgot to check. I was in a rush."

Yuna was harsh toward her mother. Yuna is a planner and a doer; her frustration with her mother's somewhat slow and easy-going manner was understandable. She is a lot like her father, Tsuyoshi.

"Is there anything you want?" Fumiko asked.

"No, I need you to sign some papers for school tomorrow. I'll leave them on the table. I'm going back to bed. Good night." With that, Yuna hung up the phone.

For her part, Fumiko wanted to talk to her daughter about her work, her boss and all kinds of other things. But she understood that her daughter was preoccupied with her own life, her own worries. Yuna doesn't have space in her life to be a sounding board for her mother.

Given the circumstances, Fumiko has to thank her daughter for standing by her all this time.

Fumiko was thirty-five when she met Yuichi. Yuna was in sixth grade. Yuichi was a teacher at a cram school where Yuna did extra studies.

Yuichi was the quiet type. He was thorough in his teaching, but he never flattered or interfered with his students. He could be strict at times, especially when it really mattered. The students liked him — he was sort of like a reliable big brother.

Yuichi spent his childhood in the US. He traveled back and forth between Japan and Canada in his adult years. He spoke English fluently and he dressed more casually than his colleagues, yet he didn't have the flair of someone who had just returned from living overseas. If anything, "taciturn" would be the right word to describe him. He was previously a teacher at a major English language school. He also served as a school placement counselor for overseas returnees at his current cram school.

To be honest, Yuichi's quiet and thoughtful personality was so diametrically opposed to that of her husband that when she first talked to Yuichi, she was concerned about his effectiveness as a teacher.

Tsuyoshi was a director at a television station. He was dedicated to his job. From the time he spent toiling in a local branch up until this day, he had never veered from the path of broadcast journalism. With every job transfer (and there were many), the family packed up their belongings and moved. Yuna spent several years living in London. Worried about Yuna's education, Fumiko returned with Yuna to Japan before she started middle school.

That explains why Yuna was enrolled in a cram school with a counselor who specializes in helping returnees assimilate into the Japanese school system. Fumiko was happy to enroll Yuna into any school as long as it suited her daughter's personality and was easy to get into. But Tsuyoshi had other ideas. He was adamant that Yuna shoot high. Yuna was a rather serious student and smart, like her father. As soon as they returned to Japan, Yuna's grades improved quickly, bringing her close to the top of the class. The relaxed and comfortable atmosphere of the cram school had helped, and Yuna made a lot of friends. In meetings with Fumiko, Yuichi told her, "Yuna attended a local school overseas long enough to qualify for returnee status in examinations. She should be able to get into a reputable middle and high school of her choice."

Fumiko had completely forgotten about Yuichi ever since that meeting. Schooling was no longer an issue because of Yuna's good grades, plus, Yuichi didn't leave much of an impression. So one day that year when Yuichi approached her at a middle school sporting event, for a moment Fumiko didn't even recognize him.

"Aren't you Yuna's mother?"

Fumiko turned around to see Yuichi smiling. "I didn't know cram-school teachers showed up at middle school," she said.

"The children wanted me to come today. Is Yuna's father here?"

For a second, Fumiko fumbled for an answer. Sports Day is held on a Sunday, which makes it easy for fathers to attend. There were times when Fumiko wished Tsuyoshi were here. But her workaholic husband rarely showed up at Yuna's school events even when he lived in Japan, and Yuna was used to her father's absence. On the rare occasions when Tsuyoshi returned home, Fumiko could see that Yuna got a little nervous. With just two women living together, life can be easy. In fact, the two of them have gotten so used to the pace they've created, Tsuyoshi's presence could be stifling.

"My husband works overseas," Fumiko replied.

"Oh I see. I thought he had returned from overseas a year ago."

"Only Yuna and I returned. My husband stayed on in London."

"That's quite a distance. It must be hard on both of you."

Yuichi became very quiet after that. He was not much of a conversationalist.

To fill in the awkward silence, Fumiko said quickly, "But he was always a busy man. Even when he lived here, he rarely came to his daughter's school events. We're used to living without him — it's really not that tough." She sounded so defensive! Soon she was feeling self-conscious.

Fumiko doesn't remember how their romance grew after that day. What she remembers is that it was a crisp, sunny day, perfect for Sports Day; that Yuichi turned out to be easy to talk to despite her self-consciousness; and that they were the same age and they both liked the outdoors. They exchanged cellphone numbers that day. Several days later, Yuichi called Fumiko and asked her out for tea. After several dates having tea and watching movies, fragments of their lives started coming together. And yet, their relationship remained platonic. They never held hands; they just hung out together, strolling through the city like middle-school kids on a date. It took almost a year before they became more than just friends. The slow transition from friends to lovers seemed like an inevitable, natural one. Fumiko was not necessarily looking for a lover, and Yuichi was not looking for a steamy love affair with a married woman. Unlike her somewhat inequitable relationship with her husband, Fumiko's relationship with Yuichi was a friendly one between equals.

Tsuyoshi was a man who pursued and gained financial and societal success. Yuichi, on the other hand, was still single at thirty-five, had never been married, and after hopping from one job to the next, landed work as a cram school teacher — not exactly a stable job. From a societal standpoint, many women would hesitate before marrying a man like Yuichi, Fumiko thought.

He was also a bit too carefree for even laid-back Fumiko. He was careless about money and relationships. Before he met Fumiko, Yuichi was dating a dancer from the Philippines. She didn't ask him how they met or what type of relationship they had, but through bits and pieces of information, Fumiko learned that she had borrowed more than a million yen from him and returned to the Philippines. "I considered that money a gift, not a loan," Yuichi said with some hesitation. The fact that she left him seemed to have shaken him more than the unreturned cash. It was a loss that took him years to recover from.

At the time, Fumiko felt sorry for him and always picked up the tab when they went out. Whenever it was time to settle the bill and Fumiko pulled out her wallet, Yuichi would say "thank you" without hesitation. Those were the times when he looked more like an easy-going Canadian than a Japanese. In time, however, Fumiko began to question his behavior. Hadn't he, after all, spent all kinds of money on his previous girlfriend? After a while, Fumiko decided to be direct with Yuichi.

"You know what? I really don't mind paying for you, but

this is not exactly coming from my own earnings. My husband worked hard to earn this," she said.

Fumiko could never even dream of being this direct with her husband, but for some reason, she could just say things to Yuichi. What was more surprising was Yuichi's reaction. He didn't argue. He just looked down and apologized. He remained quiet for a long time. Fumiko thought he was crying. They parted that day without saying a word.

Yuichi never let Fumiko pick up the tab again.

FUMIKO HAD never worked a day since getting married. She was a typical full-time homemaker. The only exception to that was a weeklong part-time job she held sorting New Year's postcards at the post office. That was the year Fumiko began dating Yuichi, and she wanted to buy him a Christmas gift with her own money. Yuichi was not a Christian, but he seemed to put more weight on Christmas than New Year's because of the time he had spent living overseas. Buying Yuichi a gift with her husband's earnings seemed too uncouth — even if her husband knew nothing about it. After all, Fumiko had her pride.

The work itself was simple — just sorting postcards by serial number. She worked among high school students and foreigners who spoke very little Japanese. Although nothing about the job was complex, Fumiko was so tense that she could barely eat lunch for the first two days. This is what happens when one stays out of the work force for more than a decade, Fumiko thought.

Fumiko didn't have any specific future plan that involved Yuichi at that point, but she did have some vague fantasies about their life together. The week she spent at the post office served as a wake-up call, making her realize how infantile her dreams were. Instead of feeling confident and happy about earning her own money, she only felt dread — dread at the numerous hardships the future was sure to bring. The experience scared her into seeking some form of employment.

Fumiko's husband returned about a year and several months after that Sports Day event — just when Fumiko and Yuichi's friendship was transitioning into a deeper romantic relationship. On the outside, nothing about Fumiko appeared to be that different from before. She mindlessly tended to housework and performed her role as a mother, while Tsuyoshi, as usual, kept busy with work, coming home only to sleep. Her meetings with Yuichi became scarce, but then Yuichi was not the type of guy to make demands of Fumiko. Fumiko had no desire to divorce Tsuyoshi and begin a new life with Yuichi. But she was certain that their affair had a profound and lasting impact on her, one that had caused a fundamental change inside of her.

Fumiko had not necessarily tired of Tsuyoshi. She respected him as a human being and even thought that she could never really dislike him. As a journalist, Tsuyoshi hated anything crooked; he was always on the side of justice. His goals were clear, and he worked hard to achieve them. He was an indomitable spirit. He drank alcohol with an insatiable thirst and smoked more than a pack of cigarettes a day. In Japan, he rarely returned home before midnight. One could say he was too serious, but he had the trust and respect of many. He was a man who derived his pride from his work. Tsuyoshi seemed larger than life to Fumiko. Sometimes she wondered if the word "hero" was created to describe the man she married.

However, Tsuyoshi also had an answer for everything. His response could be summarized as: "Who do you think puts food on the table?" He considered providing his family with financial protection an important priority, but in other family matters, he showed very little interest.

That side of Tsuyoshi was shaped by his upbringing, according to Fumiko.When Tsuyoshi was still in middle school, his father's business got saddled with a huge debt that led to bankruptcy. Tsuyoshi's parents, Tsuyoshi himself and his brother fell on hard times. Tsuyoshi attended high school part time and went to college on a scholarship. He managed several part-time jobs through college, paying his way through school.

It was around this time that Fumiko met Tsuyoshi. Fumiko had had a comfortable upbringing. Her father worked for a major manufacturing company, making him a member of the elite corps of businessmen at the time. Coming from a relatively well-to-do family, Fumiko knew next to nothing about money troubles. But when it came to education, her parents were very strict. She was practically forced to go to a girls' high school — she didn't even consider raising an objection. Tsuyoshi was her first boyfriend in college; Fumiko had never been held by anyone else. Tsuyoshi seemed so much older and mature than her, although they were the same age. He was a strong man — he never whined or showed any weakness.

Right before graduating from college, when Tsuyoshi landed a job at a local news bureau, Fumiko's father called upon him and told him that he had until his twenty-fifth birthday to finalize decisions regarding his daughter. Tsuyoshi surprised Fumiko's father by responding: "That means I can have Fumiko?" Their engagement was virtually sealed right there without any regard for Fumiko's feelings. Fumiko worked briefly after graduating from college, but a year later she moved to Tsuyoshi's place to get married. By twenty-four, she was a mother.

On the surface, their married life was serene, with very few arguments. Tsuyoshi's work constantly kept him away from home. As far as Fumiko knew, he never had an extramarital affair and for twelve years, until she met Yuichi, Fumiko never disobeyed her husband. When they lived in London, they hired a maid to clean the house once a week. Fumiko had never had to work a day since their marriage. She was ensured a comfortable life.

After having a child, they rarely had sex, but it didn't bother her. "Most couples are probably like that," she thought and quickly dismissed it. But then, it wasn't a topic she discussed with her friends, so how was she really to know what sort of sex life most couples had? Sometimes she would glance at a woman's magazine that featured the sex lives of other married couples, but perhaps it's her dispassionate nature — she was not that interested in sex.

At first, she didn't understand how she ended up where she was. Her relationship with Yuichi was clearly different from what she had with Tsuyoshi. Fumiko felt that she was fulfilled in her relationship with her lover — both in spirit and body. But the more fulfilled she felt, the greater her sense of guilt at betraying her family. She knew that she could never be forgiven for what she was doing. Fumiko was not interested in brand-name goods or shopping — typical pastimes of many housewives married to foreign correspondents. What mattered most to Fumiko was having a husband who could comfortably support her, and Tsuyoshi was that man.

It would be a lie to say that life with such a man presented no problems. Fumiko's definition of a secure life was merely a framework called "family" that her strict father had created and passed on to her husband, who now managed it. The manager had simply changed hands, but Fumiko's status as a tenant within that framework hadn't changed at all. As long as Fumiko continued abiding by the rules laid out by the manager, she suffered no inconveniences. It was as comfortable as a lukewarm bath. She never felt the need nor the desire to leave that environment. And yet, Fumiko recalls that deep down inside, she felt that she was under her husband's control. Was she just trying to be a "good girl" in front of her father and husband? Was she a good wife to her husband because she was afraid of living on her own? It was not really a marriage of false pretenses, but Fumiko felt that she had never revealed her true feelings to her husband.

Fumiko consulted a divorce counselor about six months after Tsuyoshi returned from London. For the past six months, she suppressed a growing discontent within her. She could no longer live this lie. It was several months before she could summon up the courage to contact the counselor she had found on the Internet.

The business card read: Divorce Counselor — Yoko Nomura. According to her website, Nomura was a divorcee herself and claimed she could educate women on how to get what they wanted out of a divorce. At first glance, Nomura, in her sharp-looking business suit and manicured nails, looked like she might be in her early fifties or younger.

After exchanging platitudes, Nomura leaned toward Fumiko and asked, "So how can I help you?" Fumiko told her everything — that she had a lover and her husband was not to blame, that she had no immediate plans to live with her lover, but that she was finding it increasingly difficult to stay in the marriage like nothing was happening. After Fumiko poured her heart out, Nomura paused and asked her: "And what do you want to do about it?"

"What do I want to do about it? I feel bad for my daughter. She's in middle school. I don't know, perhaps I should just suck it up and live with it. But I feel terrible about living this lie toward my husband and daughter ..."

"Do you work?"

"No."

"Are you looking for work?"

"No, not yet."

After letting out a rather exaggerated sigh, Nomura said, "Do you know what it means to get a divorce? You're talking about feeling guilty and all, but getting a divorce is like stepping into hell. If you're not working, shouldn't you be placing your priority on how to settle a divorce to your advantage?"

Nomura looked straight into Fumiko's eyes with a razor-sharp gaze that reminded Fumiko of a lawyer, not a counselor. It was as if she were being scolded by her mother; she shrank like a little girl before this counselor.

"Yes, that's true, but I am the one who is betraying my husband. My husband is probably not even having an affair," Fumiko said.

"Excuse me for being direct, but are you having sex with your husband?" Nomura suddenly asked.

"No, not often," Fumiko said, stumbling over her answer to the unexpected question.

"By 'not often' you mean you haven't had sex with him in years, correct?"

"Yes."

"In other words, your sex life is void. And you believe that your husband has never betrayed you sexually?"

At that moment, Fumiko felt the blood leave her face. The belittling manner in which Nomura spoke of her husband infuriated her. Fumiko quickly reminded herself that she was here to receive consultation on divorcing that very man. She felt light-headed when she realized that Nomura was on her side, even if she appeared to be an enemy, and that her husband was the real enemy in the coming divorce hell.

"Do you know what 'divorce by spouse of fault' means?"

Nomura pretended not to notice Fumiko's expression. "For a long time after the war, the Japanese Supreme Court upheld the ruling that the spouse who created the grounds for divorce cannot seek one. The decisive case was in 1952. A married man had an extramarital affair that ended up in pregnancy. He separated from his wife and began living with his lover. The man sought a divorce from his wife, but the Court ruled that the husband's behavior was too selfish. Ever since then, the idea that a spouse who had an extramarital affair could initiate a divorce was considered unethical. What reversed that trend was a 1987 Supreme Court ruling, which also involved an extramarital affair. But in this case, the husband sought a divorce thirty-six years after he began living with his lover. The Court granted him his wish — although he was the one at fault — simply because so much time had passed since then. This case changed the course of legal rulings. From then on, the spouse at fault has only been able to seek a divorce if he or she has been living with a lover for a certain number of years, no small children are involved and the case doesn't ostentatiously clash with social mores. When all those conditions are met, some divorces initiated by the spouse at fault have been granted. These are the exceptions to the rule. In general, many divorces initiated by the spouse at fault are still not granted.

"Let's apply this to your case. So far, your husband may not be aware of your affair, but if it ever comes to a divorce, he will probably hire a private detective, which means there's no guarantee your affair will remain confidential. If you are serious about seeking a divorce, you have to start getting rid of everything and anything that could be used against you in court. Emails, cellphone call histories — these are places we often leave tracks. Never initiate a confession. If he doesn't know, then good. That's where you want him to be.

"Also, if you want to seek a divorce, keep your reasons clear.

If your husband is not to blame, you will still have to search everywhere to find that blame. Even by manipulation, question him until he admits to just one extramarital affair, then record it. There are women who hide little microphones inside their bras and make their husbands confess to an affair. That's how prepared you have to be to win a case."

Nomura continued explaining the cases she had handled as Fumiko silently listened. They involved checking the husband's incoming and outgoing cellphone calls, hiring private detectives — and that was just the beginning. Some wives had fabricated evidence. In some cases, the wives themselves were having affairs. "Strike before he finds out," said Nomura, explaining the merits of that philosophy at length. "That's how you get what you want out of a divorce."

Fumiko paid the ten thousand yen counseling fee and stepped out of the office. The sky was an almost blinding blue. The trees in the park were swaying in the breeze. Fumiko thought that she would never return to this office. She had no intention of hating and holding a grudge against Tsuyoshi. She respected him as a human being. But if asked whether there was any love left in their marriage, the answer would be no. Nomura helped Fumiko realize that.

Fumiko wondered. How does one decide when a couple's marriage has broken down? If the basis for that is the last day they had sex, when exactly was that? No matter how hard she tried, Fumiko couldn't remember the last day she slept with Tsuyoshi. It pained her that she couldn't remember what now seemed to her like a very important day, and she cried.

Fumiko's session with Nomura was so unpleasant that it sent chills through her body. The session did achieve one thing, though: it helped her realize that there was no turning back. From that day on, Fumiko's life took a dramatic turn. Fumiko discarded most of what Nomura had told her except for one thing: she decided that she would never confess to her husband about her infidelity, not because it would serve her better in the event of a possible divorce, but because preserving his self-respect was the least she could do to atone for her sins. If Tsuyoshi found out on his own, backed by unmistakable evidence, then she would apologize. For Tsuyoshi, a man with a fierce sense of pride, learning that another man had taken his wife would be an embarrassment of unbearable proportions. His wife's disloyalty would bring shame to the entire family. By confessing, Fumiko may be able to reduce her feelings of guilt, but what good would it do for Tsuyoshi?

Shortly afterward, Fumiko told Tsuyoshi that she wanted a separation. She told him that they were emotionally incompatible. Fumiko detected what seemed like a faint smile on his face as he said: "Emotionally incompatible? What sort of nonsense are you talking about?"

Tsuyoshi probably didn't think Fumiko was serious. He never discussed emotions. Instead, he threw out a slew of questions as if he were an interrogator: "If you leave this house, where are you going to go?" and "How are you going to live when you don't even have a job?" When she replied that she would rent an apartment and find a job, Tsuyoshi said, "Fine, go ahead and do it if you think you can." Perhaps he expected Fumiko to give up and return after a while. Either way, Tsuyoshi maintained his poise throughout. The only thing he insisted on was that he pay her rent and that the family get together once a week for the sake of their daughter.

Fumiko made all the arrangements for the move. Afraid of becoming too emotional, she didn't tell Yuichi about it. She didn't want to give him the impression that the move was for him. When she told him after she had moved, Yuichi said, "Why didn't you tell me? I could've helped."

That was two years ago. The first thing Fumiko did after the move was look for work. Fortunately, being an English literature major in university and her experience living in London helped her land a job at a temp agency that specialized in foreign companies. She got the job with very little fanfare. Her first assignment was at the administrative division of a major foreign firm.

Temp workers rarely work overtime, are paid a better hourly wage than regular employees and can go home at a decent hour. But without a bonus and a regular pay raise, a temp worker's annual income ends up being more than one million yen less than that of a full-time employee. No work means no income, so in May, during the Golden Week holidays, and around New Year's, Fumiko's income disappeared. Without a regular pay raise, Fumiko sensed an invisible line that separated her from her full-time colleagues. Fumiko was never given any work with responsibility.

Just when she was beginning to feel insecure about her future, her boss at the foreign firm asked her one day, "Aren't you worried about your future? I'm thinking about switching jobs. Would you be interested?" And that's how she left her temp job for something more secure.

Her new workplace was full of young women. A few insults targeted at her when she first began working didn't bother her. A woman gains a certain peace of mind when she passes the age of forty. Because she gained full-time status at work, Fumiko no longer had the freedom she enjoyed as a temp worker. She often worked overtime and stumbled home around midnight. Perhaps because of that, her shoulders were constantly stiff, and suddenly one day, she couldn't raise her right arm. She went to see a doctor who told her that her ligaments were inflamed and she should rest for two weeks. There was no way she could take so much time off from a job she had just landed. She took one day off, swallowed painkillers and returned to work the next day.

Tsuyoshi still wouldn't consent to a divorce. The separated couple got together with Yuna every weekend at Fumiko's apartment for dinner. Fumiko called it a "banquet." At this banquet, which became almost ritualistic, Tsuyoshi would ask Yuna about school and Yuna would respond. It was the same pattern every week. Yuna, an adolescent, viewed her father as a bit of an annoyance, but being the honor student that she was, she politely responded to each question he asked. Tsuyoshi, with a beer in one hand while enjoying Fumiko's home cooking, listened carefully to his daughter. When the conversation died out, he would reach for the TV remote and toggle back and forth between sports and news. Tsuyoshi used to say, "Because of my work, I'm interested in what other TV stations are showing." His TV viewing habits hadn't changed one bit. Time floated by at these weekly banquets as if nothing had changed. The only difference was that at the end of dinner, Tsuyoshi left to go home.

Tsuyoshi had never asked Fumiko whether she was seeing another man. As far as Fumiko could tell, he hadn't unleashed a private detective on her or followed her around. But when Fumiko brought up the topic of divorce, all Tsuyoshi would say was, "I'll think about it." Fumiko could never tell what went through Tsuyoshi's mind.

Yuichi, on the other hand, had been giving Fumiko 100,000 yen in cash every month ever since she left Tsuyoshi's house. Yuichi called it a little "gift from the heart." Fumiko was grateful for the gift, but she never touched it, even during months when money was tight. She stashed all of it into a savings account. If they should ever break up, Fumiko planned on returning everything to Yuichi. She wanted to be clear that she was not seeing him for his money.

❁

FIVE YEARS have passed since she first met Yuichi. Fumiko still likes Yuichi as much as she did when they first began dating. But between work, raising a daughter and housework, Fumiko has little time to give him. She has spent so much time battling her insecurities about their future and money that Fumiko no longer knows what to think about her relationship with him.

When Fumiko came home from work today, the door to Yuna's bedroom was shut. She glanced over at the dining table and found a printout that read: Notice for Parents' Meeting. Fumiko checked the little box next to the phrase "will not attend" and stamped her name on it. Ever since taking on full-time work, Fumiko has rarely attended PTA meetings at Yuna's school. PTA programs are often held on weekday afternoons. Working mothers have to take days off to attend. Lately, Fumiko knows little about who Yuna's teachers are and what sort of academic and social life her daughter leads. She feels lonely, disconnected from her daughter in ever-increasing degrees. Having said that, high school-age children tend to distance themselves from their parents. Fumiko worries that spending so little time with her daughter will have some sort of negative repercussions. She can't help but wonder how all this will affect Yuna in her adulthood. Sometimes she has trouble sleeping at night as she ponders that question. Deep down inside, Fumiko is racked with guilt that she hasn't been a good mother to Yuna.

And yet, Fumiko is resolved to keep her chin up and move forward. Just a few years ago, all she could do was sort postcards at the post office. Now she has an apartment, albeit a small one, and is running her own life. Sometimes she feels like she should give herself a pat on the back. Yuna might consider that a selfish act, but Fumiko has no regrets, regardless of what anybody says

— at least that's what she tells herself.

Fumiko washes the rice and sets the timer on the rice cooker for six AM so she can make Yuna's lunch tomorrow. She opens the refrigerator to check the contents and decides to make Yuna's favorite: ginger-flavored minced chicken on rice. She glances at the clock. It's already past midnight. ❂

THE SEX VOLUNTEER

Hideo Sasaki, IT Salesman, 44

HIDEO SASAKI is a forty-four-year-old executive at one of Japan's most successful information-technology firms. He wears a handsome Japanese-brand suit and tie, a noted divergence from the more extravagant Armanis favored by many in his industry. He does not dye his hair — the grey shines naturally in the sunlight.

Mr. Sasaki was promoted to head one of the company's sales divisions a few years ago. He considers himself an effective worker and says he is proud that his accomplishments are recognized by the company.

Mr. Sasaki is also the father of three children ranging in age from five to twelve. On weekends, he is the Good Dad, playing and hanging out with his kids as much as possible.

Mr. Sasaki provides for his family: they own a house in an upper-middle-class neighborhood outside of Tokyo. His monthly paycheck is deposited directly into his wife's account, a Japanese tradition of sorts where the wife oversees the household finances. Mr. Sasaki considers himself a good father, and he calls himself a "good enough" husband. Not perfect by any means, but "good enough."

But Mr. Sasaki leads a double life. When he is not playing the role of Good Dad, Accomplished Executive or "Good Enough" Husband, he is a Sex Volunteer. He has slept with at least 100 women in the last three years, he says. The youngest was twenty-four and the oldest was sixty-two. The experience has made him something of an expert in female sexuality and the psychology behind it, he relates with evident pride.

Some of his lovers are married; others are single. Some are skinny, others fat. He takes pride in his performance, satisfying each and every one of them, a perfect male stud with a perfect erection regardless of his personal predilections. Like a Zen master, he never wavers when performing his task. He listens attentively as his clients talk on and on about their loveless, sexless lives; he consoles them and encourages them when necessary; then he takes them to a hotel to work his magic.

Sometimes he plays the role of marriage counselor. Other times, he acts like a gynecologist. Once, he helped a woman in her forties discover that she suffered from uterine cancer, he says. "When I touched her, I felt something was wrong. I told her to go see a doctor immediately, because it may be a myoma or something. A few days later, she was diagnosed with cancer. She thanked me for that and for giving her one last orgasm before her uterus was removed," Mr. Sasaki recalls. He grins when asked how he could diagnose such a thing without being a doctor. "Having slept with more than one hundred women, I could easily tell the difference, couldn't I?"

Being a salesman, Mr. Sasaki works long, grueling hours, but he has a certain degree of flexibility in his schedule. When the overtime hours have piled up or he works on a holiday, he is given a weekday off as compensation. On those days, he leaves his home as usual, wearing his conservative business suit. But instead of going to work to manage his sales division, he turns into Hide-san, a casual nickname his clients use for him, and offers his services to lonely women looking for sex. Hide-san is not a prostitute—no money changes hands, and his services are completely voluntary.

On one typical morning for Hide-san, he meets a woman for breakfast followed by a juicy couple of hours in a love hotel. After saying his good-byes, he heads to an early lunch with another woman, which is followed by another physical session in a city hotel. He meets another woman at three in the afternoon, then another at six, then heads home after a long day of volunteer work.

Almost all of these appointments require "full course meals," Hide-san says, using the phrase to connote both dating and sex. His clients expect him to function no matter how busy he is, he says, so he takes vitamin C supplements, drinks two liters of water a day and occasionally turns to an energy drink or a garlic extract to keep him going.

During sex, he tries to keep from ejaculating in order to be ready for the other women on his itinerary. But some women demand that he come when they climax. He says he secretly enjoys sex with these women—the ones with the healthy sexual appetites—although he tries hard not to get too personal. He wants to be fair to everyone.

Hide-san, or Mr. Sasaki, is a registered volunteer at a sex clinic in a Tokyo suburb run by Mr. Kim Myongan. Mr. Sasaki had to go through several rounds of interviews, as all the volunteers do.

Mr. Kim is not a doctor. He is a fifty-four-year-old anthropologist who specializes in sexology. He has lectured at Kyoto Seika University and has published extensively on the topic of sex. Mr. Kim began his work as a sex therapist on a radio show back in the 1980s. Listeners would call in and ask him all sorts of sex-related questions.

During his several years at the radio station, it dawned on him that many women were locked in sexless marriages. Out of desperation, they would often turn to fortune-tellers for advice. Mr. Kim would tell his female listeners that there was nothing wrong with their sexual desires, there was nothing to be ashamed of. But many women tended to blame themselves for "wanting more sex than they think they deserve," Kim explained.

The more he talked to women and provided on-air counseling on his radio show, the more Mr. Kim was convinced that a large cross-section of Japanese women were leading sexually frustrated lives. In 1999, he opened his sex clinic to help some women end their frustration.

Mr. Kim's clinic has treated hundreds of clients. In 2004, for example, about two hundred people visited his clinic. About forty of them were single females who were either virgins or very inexperienced sexually. As many as ten men used the clinic as well. The rest — the great majority — were housewives trapped in sexless marriages. They ranged in age from their early thirties to well into their sixties.

Couples who don't have sex for five, ten years are not uncommon in Japan, Mr. Kim says. Some of the women visiting the clinic say they haven't had sex in fifteen years. Many women married young and were sexually inexperienced. They were often married to well-off, socially successful men — the sort of men Japanese girls dream about marrying. But often, Kim explains, once the wife has given birth to a child or two, the men lose interest in having sex.

Mr. Kim relates the story of a young woman who had a *dekichatta kekkon*, or a marriage when she was already pregnant. She told Mr. Kim that she and her husband had never again had sex in their ten years of marriage. Japan's Health Ministry reports that the so-called dekichatta kekkon phenomenon accounts for twenty-five percent of all Japanese marriages. Mr. Kim suspects that some of these couples may end up not having sex with each other at all during their married lives.

"The problem is that once a couple gets married and has a child or two, the husband loses sexual interest in his wife. He starts treating her like his mother," Mr. Kim says. He attributes this to what he calls "the immature male psychology" predominant among Japanese men. "Mature men are hard to find in Japan. They can't let go of their image of mother as the ideal woman. For them, women are either mothers or lovers, and many say making love to their wives feels like incest," Mr. Kim says.

So do these men have more affairs to make up for their sexless marriages? Mr. Kim says that is not necessarily the case. He figures only about ten percent of the men in sexless marriages do. But others watch pornographic videos openly at home and masturbate along to them, sometimes with their wives in the next room, he says. "What do you think goes through a wife's head while her husband is beating off to a triple X movie but not even touching her? Wouldn't she feel betrayed and hurt?" Kim asks. "Of course she does."

What complicates the problem further, Kim says, is that these men are often seen as nice guys. They are comfortable in social settings, they work hard, and they make good money. They are also popular among their colleagues and very self-composed. Mr. Kim argues, however, that they are mostly just good at avoiding confrontation; they are emotionally frail and afraid of getting hurt, but at home, when the colleagues are gone, they are good at manipulating their wives and making the lack of sex the wife's problem.

Mr. Kim sketches the following scenario: A wife finally works up the gumption to confront her husband about their sexless marriage; the husband, in turn, blames her. "What's the matter with you?" he may say. "I work hard to support the family, while you are having all these dirty thoughts."

Mr. Kim says about one-third of his clients have seen a doctor or psychiatrist before coming to his clinic. When the lack of sex becomes a problem in a marriage, a woman typically goes to a doctor because she gets physically run down and depressed. But doctors can only prescribe temporary remedies like tranquilizers, sleeping pills or anti-depressants. Counselors are also largely ineffective, because the topic is rarely probed and little is known about the deeper psychology of female sexuality in Japan.

Mr. Kim says the typical advice women get from professional doctors and counselors boils down to:

» *Lack of sex isn't going to kill you. Let it go.*
» *Why not divert that energy toward a new hobby?*
» *Perhaps you should try talking to your husband about this.*

Mr. Kim says his clinic deals with plenty of virgins in their forties. Many have had bad sexual experiences earlier in life that have made them afraid of men; others simply have not been able to develop an intimate relationship with a man. As they reach a certain age, they start to wonder if they will die with their virginity intact. They worry, but simply don't know what to do.

Mr. Kim tells these women what doctors and counselors don't: go and seek sexual pleasure. "I see my work as kind of a rehabilitation program," he says. "These women are seriously hurt and feel rejected because of their sexlessness. They blame themselves. They are often unsure about their own sexuality. What I do first is ask them whether they are thinking of divorcing their husbands. If that is the case, I refer them to experts who can deal with that problem. Otherwise, I let these women explore different possibilities, enjoy their lives again and regain their self-confidence and dignity."

Mr. Kim charges twenty thousand yen (about US$170) for the first session. This payment also serves as an annual fee of sorts. Mr. Kim's files are not computerized; they're kept in two sketchbooks—one contains details about the clients and one describes the volunteers. Each file contains personal information about the client or volunteer, including photos and detailed descriptions of their sexual preferences. He tries to match the clients to the best volunteer and will introduce each woman to as many as three volunteers. The women call the volunteers from his office at first (for moral support, he says), but then it is up to them to contact the volunteers on their own. The only other rule is that the cost of a date is shared by the volunteer and the client. Other than that, Mr. Kim says, he expects people to act like adults.

For his virgin clients, he has special volunteers with smaller penises who are experienced in dealing with first-timers. For those who are fearful of men and sex, he introduces a sexual massage therapist, an impotent man who knows many techniques for satisfying women.

Mr. Kim insists that his clinic is neither a dating service nor a front for male prostitutes. First, volunteers are forbidden from charging a fee. And second, Mr. Kim says he carefully selects his volunteers to find men really interested in helping women enjoy sex.

When Mr. Kim placed an ad for sex volunteers in 2002, he says he received more than one hundred applications. They were all asked to give a detailed report of their sexual history, the size of their erect penises, the total number of times they've had sex, the number of partners they've had and their favorite sexual techniques. Then the most qualified candidates were invited to a one-day training session on how women want to be treated by their sex volunteers. The trainees were then reviewed by an eight-member panel of experts that consisted of professional therapists, sex volunteers and women who have used the volunteers' services.

The panel—made up of five women and three men—asked each applicant several questions in order to determine the following:

- *Are these volunteers sexually attractive?*
- *Are they willing to put the woman's needs first and foremost and not worry about their own sexual desires?*
- *Are they financially stable? (Only men with stable incomes are accepted; they are considered less likely to turn their volunteer work into prostitution.)*

The panel works to get rid of gigolos, playboys and men who frequently sleep with prostitutes. As of 2006, Mr. Kim had about fifty sex volunteers. He's not searching for new ones, because he prefers to keep his trusted stable of volunteers around for as long as possible. As they gain experience with women, he says, they become better at their job.

Mr. Kim claims that about ninety-five percent of the women who walk through his clinic doors end up meeting one or two sex volunteers. That's why they come to the clinic in the first place, he asserts. If they come back, he charges ten-thousand yen for a one-hour session, two-thousand yen for ten-minute phone sessions and five-thousand yen per email correspondence. He says most of his clients "graduate" the clinic within a year.

Mr. Kim does not know what becomes of his clients after they leave his clinic. But he says that based on the letters he receives many have learned how to find good sexual partners or how to deal with their sexless lives.

❀

WHEN MR. SASAKI was accepted as a registered volunteer at Mr. Kim's sex clinic, he was one happy guy. In fact, he says, that's how most of the volunteers feel. They have access to all these women, and they don't have to pay a yen for them.

"But, I feel differently about my volunteer work now. What motivates me is a sense of mission."

Mr. Sasaki has a name for the phase he sees women go through once they feel they are getting too old to enjoy their sexuality and want to blossom one last time. He calls it the "dried-flower syndrome." Sex is only one part of it: they want someone to listen; they want to have a date; and they want to be recognized and treated as women, he says. For them, a sex volunteer is the last resort. They have been rejected for years by men or have been held back by their own expectations or fears, and when they turn to a sex volunteer, they are completely out of options. If the sex volunteer turns them down or can't function in bed, that would be the end of their sex lives, he says. He imagines them thinking, "Why should my husband want me when even a sex volunteer doesn't?"

"That's why we can never fail, even if they are very fat, very ugly or physically disabled. We have to be very sensitive to their needs, while being caring and loving. This applies not only in bed but at the dining table, at a restaurant or at the bar counter," Mr. Sasaki says. What makes a sex volunteer different from other men who are simply looking for a relationship is that the volunteer has no choice over the kind of women he sleeps with. It's up to them to pick him, and he almost never says no when he receives a call from Mr. Kim's office.

Mr. Sasaki says he finds the work very rewarding. Some women break down and cry just because somebody is actually listening attentively to their stories. Some weep for joy after having sex. The sense of satisfaction he gets from seeing them happy and appreciative is much greater than the physical pleasure of having sex, he says.

Mr. Sasaki had one client—a piano teacher— who told him that she had not had sex with her husband for many years. According to him, she really wasn't interested in having sex with her husband. He had gotten lazy after they married, she told him, and she started to wonder if he married her for her money. He rarely worked and spent most of his time playing pachinko.

She told Mr. Sasaki that she was bored to death teaching kids who did not seem to care about music. Some were obviously tone deaf, and she wondered why their parents ever wanted to have them learn to play the piano to begin with. She told him that she sometimes wanted to cover her ears so she did not have to listen to the awful music the children were making.

"You know what she told me? After she slept with me and had a good time, she said the whole world turned brighter and changed its colors. She said her piano students deliver sounds with crystal clarity now. That kind of comment makes me feel proud and appreciated."

❀

LIKE MANY other men, Mr. Sasaki was looking for fun when he became a sex volunteer. More specifically, he wanted to have some exciting sexual adventures to help him cope with his own sexless marriage. His marriage has not been a very happy one, redeemed only by their children, he says. His wife, Mariko, had some medical issues and had been under treatment for infertility. In the early days of their marriage, sex, to Mr. Sasaki, was associated with the act of ejaculating into a tube on certain mornings and dropping the tube off at the doctor's on his way to work.

Their first baby was born after much struggle, but the second one came naturally. Yet, Mariko and Hideo had less and less sex over those years, and finally they settled into an existence where sex was all but left out. Maybe Mariko doesn't really like sex, he thought. It was easier for him to think this way than to ponder the alternatives. Did she still love him? Was he bad in bed?

Occasionally, Mr. Sasaki attempted to have sex with Mariko. He felt the need to prove to himself that they could still make love. On some nights, Mariko relented. On others, she refused. He was left in doubt.

One night, after their two children went to sleep, Mariko told him that she was pregnant for the third time. The news came when he least expected it. Mr. Sasaki was nonetheless happy;he loves his children. It is their existence that keeps him striving to be a good husband and father, he says.

Mariko was washing dishes when she told him the news. She had her back to him. He was at a loss for words for a moment and before he could speak, she said, without turning toward him, "What do you want me to do?"

A chill went down his spine. At first, he couldn't believe what she had said, and he wondered if it really were a question or rather a statement. Is she asking my opinion about whether we should terminate the life of our child? He felt all his efforts to hold the family together over the years collapse at that instant.

He couldn't tell what his wife was thinking. Nor did he seem to care that she may have taken his silence as indifference. He looked at the newspaper on the kitchen table, and Mariko finally announced: "Well, I might as well go ahead with this, then."

Even to this day, Mr. Sasaki does not understand why Mariko asked that question. Maybe she was not sure whether he liked having children. Maybe she was just so tired of raising their two children and couldn't bear to cope with a third. Or she might have simply been curious to hear what he would say. In any case, that was the final straw for Mr. Sasaki. Mariko became a stranger to him from that day. He still tries hard to be a good family man, he says, but when he sees their third child, he cannot help but recall the bitterness he felt on that day. The thought that this child may not have been born terrifies him; he cannot let go of it. He says he can never forgive her for having uttered those words—what do you want me to do?

Soon after that day, Mr. Sasaki started meeting women via telephone clubs, the precursor to online dating services. It was the 1980s, and telephone clubs were booming in Japan. Male clients would pay a small fee to sit in a booth and receive calls from women, who could then set up a date if they wished. Mr. Sasaki became a regular at one of those clubs and met several women.

Mr. Sasaki's policy has been not to sleep with prostitutes. He wants women to want sex as much as he wants it. In his experience, there has been no scarcity of women wanting it for free. Some of those relationships lasted for a long time—as long as seven years—others were short-lived.

Becoming a sex volunteer came naturally for Mr. Sasaki. Over time, he discovered that his role as a volunteer has major social value. Most women tell him having sex has a greater impact on women's bodies than going to esthetic salons. Most of them say their skin is rejuvenated and their breasts get bigger. They say they look younger and feel happier.

However, he sometimes wonders what becomes of these women. "One woman told me that soon after she began having sex with volunteers, her husband jumped on her after so many years of never even touching her. Perhaps she became sexier after having a few encounters. But the woman said she did not want her husband anymore. She had slept with strangers, but she just couldn't do it with her husband anymore."

Other women, he says, decided to leave their husbands. Having sex may have opened their eyes to new possibilities.

Mr. Sasaki has his own personal dilemma that may help him empathize with his clients.

"As a sex volunteer, I hear women say they feel rejected when their partners refuse to have sex with them. But they do not seem to understand that men feel hurt, too, even more hurt than women, when they are rejected by their wives."

Mr. Sasaki's life is a conundrum. He has slept with more than one hundred women, but he has yet to find a solution to his own sexless marriage. ❂

THE FIX

Yazuki Saito, Sales Promotion, 47

TWENTY-NINE MILLION YEN. That's how much I'm worth. If I die because of a disease or accident, my children get paid the maximum coverage of thirty million yen. I have a one-million-yen debt and no savings to speak of, so 29 million yen is what goes to my three children. That should be enough to get them through middle school and high school, until they become independent. That doesn't mean I can shirk my responsibilities as a parent. If I were alone, I could keel over and die, but I have children to take care of ...

I work in sales promotion at supermarkets and department stores, selling food and household items like beef, razors, beer. The work is detailed. I'm kind of proud of it — it provides a humble but comfortable livelihood for us. The supermarket is synonymous with everyday life and yet it is a backdrop to all sorts of life stories. Families, elderly couples, married couples, single customers and many other types of people converge there. The supermarket has an earthiness that I respect.

I've learned through years of experience that there's one golden rule to sales work. That is, the harder you work, the greater the rewards. It pays off when you throw yourself into it. I had acting ambitions, so I'm probably well suited to work that involves dealing with people.

But every once in a while, I'm overcome with a fierce sense of insecurity and loneliness. As a single mother, I know I have to raise my children right, stay healthy, work and be emotionally strong. I know all that. It's hard enough raising three children entering puberty, but my son, who is in middle school, has lately started refusing to go to school and becomes violent at home. My daughter clashes with him, too, these days. I think she's becoming emotionally tired. The other day, she ran out of home in the middle of the night. Fortunately, she was home by morning. But at times like these, I don't know whether I can keep my family together and protect my children.

At the same time, I want to be loved by a man, just like any other woman. If that's not possible, well, then at least I want to be held, made love to. Ever since I got a divorce ten years ago, I haven't had a single sexual encounter. When I think that my life might eventually end in this fashion, I ask myself, "What was my life about?" and feel a sorrow too unbearable to deal with.

I learned about sex volunteers about a year ago. I happened to come across a story in a magazine that discussed a new way for women to deal with sexlessness. Some people may say, "You are forty-seven years old with three children. What are you thinking?" But I think it's safer and healthier to meet someone when you both know it's about sex, rather than going through multiple men on the Internet whose backgrounds aren't all that clear.

I've had relationships with seven sex volunteers over the past six months. Not all were perfect partners, but each came with deep sexual experience, and thanks to them, I feel a little less uptight, softer. This may sound strange, but I've had the chance to experience in the past six months what normal people may experience in their youth.

Sex without love is generally considered contradictory to happiness. But then no sex and no love would be even less happy. Love is important, of course, and I want to be loved, but I don't know how to make that happen, and I've never felt that I was being loved. I've always lived this way, so I'm very much aware of the possibility of dying alone. Humans are merely male or female. We all want to be held some times, feel the warmth of another. Isn't that natural?

I've had a new outfit made, applied make-up and felt the euphoria of going on a date. The joy of having someone listen to what I have to say ... These are mundane experiences everybody has. I am amazed at the fact that they were never a part of mine.

LOOKING BACK, I've spent a good portion of my life battling with myself. Towards the end of my teenage years, I became anorexic. I'm sure there were signs well before then. I just wanted to be loved.

I suppose launching into a discussion about love would make me sound like a drama queen. But for me, to live is to express oneself, whether through acting or daily life, and I try to be conscious about expressing my innermost self. What drives me is the desire to be loved, but I don't really know how to express that. That's probably because I've never been loved sufficiently.

My parents loved me in their own special way, but my mother was a selfish and emotional person. Ever since I was a child, I spent my energy playing the role of her guardian. As a result of that, I grew up without expecting kindness from someone else.

My father was a professor of a reputable university and a man of great character. He was respected by the students and his peers. I was an only child and my father doted on me. Except, he never did understand the female side of me. He taught me to "become strong like a lone wolf" and "never kiss up to anyone."

I think my parents' relationship had cooled off at an early stage. My father was a calm and logical person. He never openly clashed with my mother, but even as a child, I sensed a growing rift between the two of them. Father didn't want to put us under any kind of financial strain, so thankfully, we've never run into money problems. But at some point, my father was never home. Next thing we knew they had separated. This happened over a very long period of time, the way erosion alters the earth's topography over time, and when we eventually noticed a difference, our family dynamics had already changed.

My mother's emotional state got worse after father left home. It became my lone job to provide my mother with emotional support. Mother rarely left my side. She was my lover, my husband and my guardian. It was bothersome at times and yet I couldn't escape from her dominion. Like identical twins sharing the same womb, we remained in an enclosure called a mother-daughter relationship and refused to step out of it. This may sound very harsh, but when my mother died several years ago, while I felt sorrow, I also felt great relief. Everything about my mother — her love, her hatred — was a tremendous burden on me.

They say anorexia is caused by one's relationship with her mother. I think that was the case with me. Now I weigh forty-seven kilograms, but at my worst, my weight dropped down to the thirties. I swallowed two hundred laxative pills once and nearly died. I realized I'd rather stop doing that to myself than die and left home at the age of twenty-six. Later, I got married and had children, and in some ways, that saved my life. When I got pregnant, I had no choice but to take good care of myself and eat well. Married life was never a happy one for me, but I am thankful that I was able to have children.

I'd never really cured myself of this eating disorder. Several years ago, I swallowed a whole bunch of diet pills, and the stimulants that were contained in those pills caused a panic attack that sent me to the hospital. I guess I could've died from that. The hospital asked about my religion and contact number just in case. Tranquilizers and trips to the neurologist have been a regular part of my life since then.

❁

IN 1997, Yasuko Watanabe, a thirty-nine-year-old woman on an elite career path, was found strangled to death in her apartment in Tokyo's Shibuya Ward. The so-called "Toden Office Lady Murder" garnered sensational media coverage because Yasuko, a woman who held an executive position with Toden,[1] worked as a prostitute by night in bustling downtown Shibuya. The media had a field day with the story about this woman, who was leading a double life. Pundits focused their debates on why Yasuko, a successful career woman, became a prostitute. Every detail of her private life was pried open for the whole country to see until the victim's family protested to the police that it was

1 Japanese abbreviation for Tokyo Electric Power Co.

an egregious violation of her privacy. Ironically, her death by strangulation had turned her into a tragic heroine of the times, drawing women with university diplomas into prostitution or perverse sexual experiences in what was dubbed the Yasuko Syndrome. A large number of women identified with Yasuko — not necessarily with what she did, but with the fact that she was trying to find ways to express her self worth, however twisted her approach was.

Amid the massive media coverage of the case, the one thing that caught my attention was not the frequency with which she engaged in bizarre behavior (weekends were spent working at masochist clubs; on weekdays she regularly took in four customers after finishing work at the power company, having sex with customers on building stairs and parking lots, urinating on the street, soiling hotel rooms with excrement and urine), but statements from witnesses that she was "devouring sweet baked goods on the street" or "openly eating on the train." Media reports said that Yasuko suffered from anorexia. She probably bought pastries at the end of her "work" in Maruyamacho. Reports back then said she was 169 centimeters tall and weighed forty-four kilograms at the time of her death. She was so hungry that she couldn't wait until she got home. The sight of an emaciated woman wolfing down bread ...

I can't help but juxtapose myself with this woman: the company I used to work for was close to the station Yasuko used to go home; the fact that her father was also a famous university professor ...

At the time, I earned a living by making sales calls over the phone to help support the family. I worked hard all day without resting for a meal, and to fill my empty stomach on the way home, I would stop at a store to buy some sweet pastries. It was probably the same store that Yasuko frequented. I think eating that bread was a ritual that made it possible for me to make that transition from work to home.

All we had in common was that we possibly ate the same pastries from the same store, and yet I feel such a strong affinity with Yasuko. I think that's because we've both lived on the edge with anorexia, living with a fear of death and the ever-present state of starvation.

I don't know if there is a psychological relationship between sexuality and anorexia. For me, though, I've always had something of a yearning for things related to prostitution. My involvement with sex volunteers might merely signal an awakening of that part of me.

The other day, when I went on a date around here with a sex volunteer, I thought about Yasuko. I think she, like me, wanted to give herself over to the pulse of a place that oozes desire.

❁

IF I WERE happily married, what would have happened? Perhaps without a recurrence of anorexia, I'd be a round middle-aged woman. But I can't picture myself that way. There's no point in looking back, so I try not to think about the past too much. With regards to marriage, I think I was too careless. It ended in divorce because it had to.

I graduated with a degree in English literature, but after I left my mother's home, I decided to go into acting and joined a theater company. That wasn't enough to earn a living, so like most actresses, I worked as a hostess at a club in Kabukicho in Shinjuku. I had never dated a man before, so I had no sexual experience.

I lost my virginity when I was twenty-six. It was very anticlimactic. I had sex with the first customer who came to the club — it was strictly business and quite unimpressive. I had no experience when it came to romance. I was also indifferent to romance probably because I was a hostess. I felt like I could see the bleak ending before it even started. It was hard to get excited about romance. That was when I met Keiichi.

Keiichi was not a regular at the club. He happened to stop by one night. He didn't strike me as especially handsome or intelligent. As someone who ran an engineering firm, he exuded a certain confidence that I found attractive. I can't remember what we discussed that evening. We just went back to my apartment. Several days later, Keiichi brought his stuff and moved into my place. Next thing I knew, we registered with the city and became husband and wife.

We didn't have a wedding.

Now that I think about it, maybe that was Keiichi's plan all along. Everything happened fast so it may appear impulsive, but he may have been thinking, "Her father's a university professor; they must have money" or something like that. Frankly, I liked the way he'd squeeze my hand and say, "Yazuki is such a hard worker." I erroneously thought that I could endure hardship with this man and find love, despite objections from my parents.

Keiichi was born to a poor family who lived in the shadows of deep snow-covered mountains. He lost both parents when they were young and came to Tokyo with his younger sister. He raised his younger brother while building up his own company, so he was a capable man. I quit my evening job and joined Keiichi's company, helping him with clerical work. I organized the invoices, kept the books in order and managed payments and client matters.

We lived in an apartment in Shinjuku at the time. The cozy apartment we shared with Keiichi's brother was always busy with people from work. Pretty soon my apartment became an office. Keiichi took good care of his people and he was generous when he had money, so he was always surrounded by people of all sorts. I, on the other hand, felt like I was being chiseled away by this lifestyle.

When I was in the hospital after miscarrying my first baby, my husband called me to "come back home because there's clerical work piling up." I told the hospital, "I really need to go back home," and took care of all the hospital paperwork on my own. When I returned home, there was a mountain of bills to organize. I was so sad ...

I gave birth to three children after that. Raising children was difficult, but they were an important part of my life. While I kept myself busy with the children, I could tell my husband's business was visibly slowing down. The Japanese economy went into a recession, plus the business was probably a bubble business. Anyway, Keiichi lost his livelihood and began playing pachinko and betting on horses. When he came home, he'd take it out on me or the children. One time he took my son, still a little child, and stuck his head in the toilet as "discipline." Our family began to disintegrate.

After a while, I moved out with my children and got a divorce. I live in a state-owned apartment for low-income families for twenty thousand yen a month. I'm surrounded by elderly people. It becomes so quiet around here during the day that you can't believe you are in the middle of the city. My work is busy on the weekends and on weekdays I tend to get days off. When I first moved out here, I couldn't stand being on my own after the children left for school. I used to decorate the walls with their calligraphy from school. The power in their brushwork was so potent that I felt as if it could get rid of all the negative energy.

Just the other day an elderly person who lived alone passed away. Group funerals are held for the dead who don't have relatives to claim them. In this wealthy nation, few places are like this. But I like state-owned housing like this, life and death co-mingling.

❁

I'VE BEEN in love a number of times after my divorce. But as soon as I showed my seriousness, they would scatter and we would never get to the point of going out. My first heartbreak was with my daughter's teacher. He seemed like a clean and polite gentleman, never made a face about attending PTA meetings. He was quite popular among the mothers. After meeting him a few times, I completely fell for him.

I went to as many PTA meetings as I could just so I could meet him. Every chance I got, I baked him home-made cookies — I never hid my feelings from him. I think my behavior made it obvious to others how much I liked him. I never liked hiding, so I continued my overtures. I was heartbroken in the end. "I'm sorry, but I can't accept your gifts," he said very politely. That was a very clear "No." I suppose dating your daughter's teacher is taboo. I was quite serious about him.

I want to give a relationship my all. But I don't know how to keep my distance with a man or how to move things along. I have no idea what I can do to make a man love me. It could be because I never had a serious loving relationship when I was young. When I found out about sex volunteers, I thought, "If I can't love properly, I should skip that whole process and jump straight into sex. That's more to the point."

I told my therapist that I was considering meeting a sex volunteer. She encouraged me. "If you think that's going to help you, by all means." There was some hesitation on my part. I finally made an appointment with the sex therapist, Kim-sensei, six months after I found that magazine article about sex volunteers.

Kim-sensei was very friendly and open. He asked me about my sexual history and preferences — what sort of sex I wanted, with what type of man, what penis size I preferred. We went through different types of men as he pointed at pictures. But I couldn't find my type through the photos. The man Kim-sensei recommended as "a fun and nice man" was sixty years old. I just couldn't find the right person and didn't know how to respond. Kim-sensei said to me, "The important thing is to garner something positive from this sexual experience. Don't rely on photos for that. The men pictured here are all kind men who can take you in." I ended up choosing a kind-looking man who was said to be a gynecologist.

"Okay, let's call him."

Kim-sensei picked up the phone, called him and handed the phone over to me. But when he answered the phone, even I could tell that my voice was shaking. I was so nervous. He told me he'd call me back to confirm the date and we hung up. It had happened so fast that I felt a little high. Kim-sensei said to me, "All's well if you can find happiness from here on in. Wear pink on the day of the date, something bright. Make it clear that you haven't given up on your sex life."

As promised, I received a call from the gynecologist a few hours later. We were to meet in a few days.

That day, I wore my suit and we met at a cafe in a city hotel at ten am. He had a bit of a paunch, but he was a gentleman, so he wore it well.

As soon as we sat down, he asked me, smiling, "What type of man do you like?" It was such a sudden question that I couldn't answer it right away, then he added, "If you can't answer a question like that right away at your age, you haven't had a lot of experience, have you? You need to have more positive experiences." He spoke in a gentle manner. I was impressed. I thought,

"Well, here's a volunteer who's had experience with dozens of women. He's perceptive." Talking to him was lots of fun; three and a half hours went by quickly.

"Well, shall we go now?" He asked nonchalantly as he stood up.

The love hotel was a clean one for a hotel in the middle of an entertainment district. I was fumbling around, unsure if I should undress myself when I looked over to see that the gynecologist was wasting no time getting undressed. He then came over to me and helped me undress. He led me to the shower and washed me well, even between my toes. In bed, he gently caressed me. I was still stiff with nervousness. I followed his lead and my experience with the sex volunteer went smoothly.

That was the only time he sleept with me. Later he told me he liked plumper women. But we went out to dinner from time to time and he'd listen to my stories. He's very kind, but he can also be brutally honest. One time I asked him, "Is it too much of me to ask a man to love me? Have I sunk too low to be loved?" "You haven't even sunk yet," he said. "You need to open yourself up to more experiences."

True, I can't argue with that. I do lack experience.

Within six months, I've slept with seven volunteers. My husband was sexually a lightweight so I didn't know sex could be this deep an experience. Some have taught and taken me to the extremes of ecstasy. But lately I've been thinking about graduating from my relationship with them.

The excitement builds up with all the email exchanges, then I raise my expectations, thinking this man might be very nice. But then we meet, and it all ends the moment our bodies touch. Our eyes barely meet when we part, walking off in opposite directions. I think I may be whittling away at myself in exchange for pleasure.

I have had fun times with these men. They took me away,

even if momentarily, from the harsh reality of my life. But I have to pay for it somehow. Sometimes I get so lonely and send out several emails to the volunteers, but when I don't hear from any one of them, I have to face the fact that I am indeed alone. Plus, going out with them has gotten me back into drinking again — something I hadn't done in ten years. When I drink, I have to stop taking my prescription tranquilizers, but if I do, I'll most definitely have another panic attack. Actually, the other day I did have one. Then I took too many tranquilizers and ended up in the hospital.

If I'm going to date strangers, then go to a hotel, I may as well make money doing that. Sometimes I think about doing that. I looked at my mounting debt and went in for an interview for a delivery health place. It is by registration only, so I have to give a certain cut to the place, which means I end up making ten thousand yen for two hours of work. I went in for the interview disappointed at the slim earnings. But I didn't get the job. I was too old and lacked experience.

I was recently asked out on a date from one of the sex volunteers, but I turned him down. I told him that I was tired of a relationship that was merely physical. For the sake of my own children, I can't continue this way. That's honestly how I feel right now. I think I'm also in love with one of the volunteers, Mokkun. He lives far away and he only comes to Tokyo once every few months, but he emails me often. When he's in Tokyo, we have dinner, go to a hotel, talk a lot — it's almost like being with a boyfriend. But he's a married man. No matter how kind he is to me, I'm still stealing somebody's husband and that depresses me sometimes. The other day, I didn't get an email response from him and did something stupid. I took a razor from the store and ran it across my wrist. I felt a sharp pain, but I didn't draw blood. Then I remembered that I was at work and tried to shift gears, but I couldn't concentrate until I received an email from Mokkun.

I want a man who would love only me. I'm finally beginning to feel a sense of normalcy returning; I'm tired of the debauched life I have led the past six months, going to hotels just to sleep with men. I would like to graduate from being someone who can only relate to men through sex. ❂

SYNCHRONICITY

Mitsuko Ishihara, Company Owner, Acupuncturist, 58

MITSUKO ISHIHARA descends her stairs at nine AM sharp to find Yuri looking over the day's schedule at Mitsuko's desk. Yuri glances at her boss out of the corner of her eye and says "good morning" without a smile. Yuri often complains that her smooth, creaseless eyelids make her look more serious than she actually is, but Mitsuko says privately that Yuri's looks are a perfect match for her personality. Mitsuko finds her assistant difficult to deal with at times; she doesn't dislike her, but Yuri's uptight energy clashes with Mitsuko's happy-go-lucky, open-minded approach. It's a karmic thing. Mitsuko imagines that they were together in past lives, perhaps as a husband and wife or a father and daughter — indispensable partners but never really close or loving.

Mitsuko lives upstairs and uses the first floor as her office. When she renovated her house to accommodate her successful home business, she was thrilled at the thought of never having to commute on those jam-packed trains again or never having to worry about covering that month's office rent. It was liberating. But now she regrets the decision. When her employees show up for work, it feels like they are invading her private space.

"Do you want a cup of coffee, *shacho*? I already made the first pot," Yuri says.

It is clear from her gesture that Yuri isn't going to fetch a cup for Mitsuko, so Mitsuko goes over to the sink and grabs her mug. The Chinese characters for shacho are written in black felt pen on the side, denoting her title as the company president. Mitsuko pours her coffee and lets out a little sigh.

Mitsuko has yet to get used to people calling her shacho, and she doesn't think she ever will. It's common in Japanese companies to call people by their titles, but Mistuko's business is small — just three full-time employees — and she feels more like a self-employed person than a company president.

Besides, if anything, she often feels more like Yuri's servant than her boss. It's in Yuri's nature to be bossy and act as if she's in charge. And Yuri doesn't seem to care much about what Mitsuko is thinking.

"Today, you have someone coming to the clinic at eleven am," Yuri says. "But I want you to return here before lunch so we can go over Mr. Yamamoto's care plan."

It's plain that Yuri doesn't approve of Mitsuko's decision to continue her acupuncture business while simultaneously running her health-care business. Yuri calls the acupuncture business "the boss' hobby." The business doesn't generate as much income as the health-care management side of things, but that's partly because the clinic where Mitsuko does acupuncture has a large mortgage payment on it. The clinic is on the first floor of a business complex along a busy thoroughfare and near a train station. Mitsuko could find a cheaper space, but her clients find the clinic convenient, and they suffer from all sorts of disabilities and ailments. To relocate and make it harder on them just doesn't feel right to Mitsuko.

During her one-hour sessions, Mitsuko is completely focused on her clients. All her energy goes to them. She considers herself more of a therapist than a businesswoman, because, after all, her health-care management business sprung out of her acupuncture work. Mitsuko loves to care for the elderly and the frail; nothing gives her more joy than to hear from a client that her treatment alleviated someone's pain.

And furthermore, Mitsuko loves the feel of human bodies.

It's not a sexual thing for Mitsuko, or even a sensual thing. It's more philosophical — she believes that humans are made up of energy and that touching brings people closer than talking could ever do. Mitsuko can distinguish good energy from bad at times just by touching someone. As she touches a client's body, she can feel the bad energy evaporating from it.

Yuri will have to learn to abide. Mitsuko will never give up her practice.

Mitsuko checks her email to see if anyone has left a message on one of her two blogs. One blog is for her business, and the other is all about her favorite Korean male singer. He is serving in the Korean military for two years but will be singing at a community event as a guest next month. Her friends in the singer's fan club have left comments on her latest posting. Many Korean stars find a way to get US citizenship and avoid military duty. But not the man she likes. He is doing his time.

His appearance at the local event was just announced recently, and his fans are writing about it all over the Internet.

One message on Mitsuko's blog has a link to a video clip of him. Mitsuko clicks and gazes at her heart-throb. "Wow, he's got a crew cut," she says to herself. It makes him look even younger and more attractive. If she takes next Friday off, she can fly to Seoul and attend his farewell party. She quickly checks available flights on the Internet. Two-night, three-day packages cost seventy thousand yen, including the hotel. It's not cheap but it's manageable, she thinks. This would be Mitsuko's eleventh trip to Korea in the last two years. Mitsuko used to spend her vacations wandering around Europe, but lately, she has joined a legion of Japanese women who have become fascinated and infatuated with South Korea.

This trend started several years ago, when a Japanese TV station began airing "Winter Sonata," a Korean drama featuring Bae Young Joon. The plot revolved around a simple love story, but there was something about this actor that drove Japanese women — especially women in their forties, fifties and sixties — wild. Thousands of women would join one of the "Winter Sonata" package tours to South Korea in hopes of getting a glimpse of him. They would visit various locations featured in the show: Yong Pyong Ski Resort and Chuncheon in the country's northern lake district. "Winter Sonata" opened the door to other Korean shows with other Korean stars. While Bae Young Joon is no longer in the limelight, the fascination with Korea and young Korean stars continues.

Sociologists have coined a phrase for this term: The Winter Sonata Phenomenon. They say Japanese women experiencing mid-life crises or stuck in loveless marriages have turned to these young Korean stars for solace.

Mitsuko doesn't know if they are right, and she's not interested in talking to her friends in the fan club about their sex lives or other personal issues. She just wants to bond with women who share the same interest: young, handsome Korean stars who exude openness, purity and warmth — attributes Japanese men are all but lacking these days, she says.

Mitsuko got caught up in this fad a little later than most of the women. She liked the sentimental presentation of director Yun Seok Ho's dramas. She had also heard that Bae had a strong aura. Out of curiosity, she joined a package tour to Oedo Island in Gyeongsangnam-do Province and another to the small east coast town of Samchok in Gangwon Province, where Bae Yong Joon's 2005 film *Outing* was shot. These tours got her hooked. Like many other women, her initial attraction to Bae ebbed, and she joined smaller groups of fans devoted to lesser-known actors and singers. These smaller groups gave her a sense of ownership: the fans feel like they've discovered their actor or singer, as opposed to following a superstar whom everyone knows.

Mitsuko fell hard for one particular Korean singer. While he was already a superstar in Korea when Mitsuko "discovered" him, he was relatively unknown in Japan. Mitsuko had to use translation software to read his website since so little information about him existed in Japanese.

Nowadays, there are several Japanese-language sites on Mitsuko's heartthrob, but she still considers herself one of his most knowledgeable fans in Japan. She secretly hopes to publish a book about him. While she is not a writer or a translator, she feels that this is her mission, based on her karma, and if she works really hard on it, it could happen.

When she is feeling anxious at work, there is nothing to take the stress away like his voice, she says. Each time she comes back from his concerts, she feels rejuvenated, ready to attend to the needs of others.

"Shacho, what do you want to do about Ms. Tanaka's care plan?" Yuri's voice jars Mitsuko from her reverie. She quickly closes her web browser so Yuri won't see that she is fantasizing about a Korean singer nearly thirty years her junior. In fact, Mitsuko realizes, she is closer to the age of his mother.

"Hmmm, let's see the plan."

"Ms. Tanaka's daughter called this morning, asking about this and that. Maybe we need to follow up with her," Yuri says.

"We can send Mr. Kinoshita to see her later this week," Mitsuko says. "Where is he anyway?"

"He said he'd be here around eleven. He is visiting a client."

Mitsuko started her company soon after Japan revised laws concerning nursing-care insurance in 2000. She started out on her own, and the business grew steadily. Her friends comment on how lucky she is to start a business in her fifties and have it grow and turn profitable in just a few years. But Mitsuko doesn't really believe it was luck — the process unfolded as it was meant to, that's all.

Mitsuko worked in an office as one of Japan's so-called office ladies until she was forty-nine. She began working at the company at the age of twenty-seven, after moving to Osaka from her hometown in the Hokuriku region, a part of Japan that is buried in deep snow at least three months of the year.

Mitsuko's father died when she was very young. Her mother raised her by herself while also running a small Japanese pastry shop. Mitsuko remembers pulling a sled through the snow to deliver the little pastries made of sticky rice and sweetened azuki beans and colored and shaped like different flowers, animals and birds. She was still in elementary school at the time. She loved that time, especially when she traveled through fresh snow, making the first imprints on the smooth, white surface. It made her feel as if she owned the world.

Mitsuko's mother didn't have to work too hard because her family was moderately wealthy. But her mother liked to keep busy. Mitsuko pitched in when she could, but she never felt a sense of urgency. She grew up in a small village, with all her relatives around her, and though she was the only child of a widowed mother, she didn't feel lonely at all. Her older cousins in the neighborhood would look out for her. Maybe this small-town upbringing was what gave Mitsuko her happy-go-lucky attitude.

Mitsuko graduated from high school and started working for a small company in her hometown. After several uneventful years there, she suddenly was struck with the urge to get out. Life in her hometown was getting too easy.

Mitsuko's mother wasn't happy about her plans to move to Osaka, but she didn't put up much resistance. A month later, Mitsuko had moved to the city with a futon and about one million yen in savings, which was a lot for a single woman in the late 1970s. Most of her friends used their savings for their weddings; Mitsuko was secretly proud that she decided to invest in her future instead.

Mitsuko found herself a small apartment in downtown Osaka and soon landed a job with a midsize trading firm. She worked eight hours a day, sometimes had dates on the weekends, would go see plays by herself on other days and often stayed in to read a book. It was a happy time for her.

After working in Osaka for four years, Mitsuko and her mother decided to pool their savings and buy a house in the city. Mitsuko's mother was ready for the move — most of her relatives had already left the snow country for Japan's second city.

Mitsuko's life in Osaka proceeded quietly for many years — she worked twenty-two years at a trading company and watched as many women joined the company, stayed a few years, then retired to get married. For Mitsuko, marriage wasn't in the cards. Sure, she had dated a few guys, but it never got serious enough to talk of marriage. One boyfriend was a doctor twelve years her senior. She was in her late twenties then, and she'd make him homemade box lunches because of his busy schedule. They dated for a year or so, but the relationship stayed platonic and eventually faded away. It was part of a pattern with her. She never had a serious relationship, not even one night in bed.

Perhaps it was because she was an only child. She has always been quite comfortable on her own. This could explain why she was a virgin until the age of fifty-two.

Or perhaps her awkward relationship with men could be tied to the fact that she matured quite early, having full breasts at the age of thirteen, something that was quite uncommon forty years ago in Japan. Mitsuko's mother worried that her well-developed daughter could attract unwanted attention from men, and Mitsuko was told time and again by her mom and other relatives to be wary of men. Mitsuko didn't really know what they were talking about — sex education was limited back then — but she developed the vague notion that men were dangerous, and perhaps that notion took root in her unconscious mind. She attended a girls' high school, too, which didn't help matters.

Or it could have been the years she spent living with her mother, caring for her at the end of her life, while others her age were out looking for Mister Right. Her mom had passed away when Mitsuko was in her mid-forties. The last years were especially tough because her mother suffered a stroke and was partially paralyzed. The stroke affected her speech, although, strangely enough, she could still sing. Mitsuko would go straight from work to the hospital and straight from the hospital to bed. Then she would wake up and repeat the cycle.

Mitsuko felt a deep sense of loss when her mother died, but she didn't cry at the funeral. She was too busy, as the only daughter, making sure the funeral and reception ran smoothly.

The sadness hit her after everything was over. She found herself alone in her house with a ceramic pot containing her mother's ashes. She crawled into her futon, wrapped herself tightly in her blankets — it felt like a cocoon — and cried violently.

Mitsuko had spent twenty-two years in her post, but she still didn't see herself as a career woman. She was a clerk, and while she was efficient and reliable, she was shuffled from department to department, which was the common practice in Japanese companies. She wasn't a certified accountant, but her skills in this field were widely acknowledged. She was once bullied by her boss and sent to another department, but that was the only trouble she remembers during her many years at the firm.

During her free time, she traveled to Europe, took yoga lessons and went to seminars on spirituality. Over time, she began to believe in synchronicity, a term coined by Dr. Carl Jung. Mitsuko came to believe that things happen for a reason even when they seem completely random and void of meaning. The universe will provide you with what is necessary as long as you open your mind to the higher energy fields. Her yoga teacher introduced new ideas like this to Mitsuko, prompting her to expand her spiritual horizons by attending meetings on spirituality and reading extensively on the subject.

Mitsuko experienced a profound breakthrough at a workshop on the book *The Celestine Prophecy* by James Redfield. Mitsuko was among the first to read the translated version of the best-selling book. Redfield's teachings were not new to her. In fact, he embraced many Asian philosophical concepts such as karma and reincarnation — concepts Asians tend to naturally believe in. Even the idea that people could be trained to see different-colored auras emanating from human bodies wasn't that surprising to her, although she had yet to advance to a state where she could see these auras herself. What empowered Mitsuko at this workshop was the idea that synchronicity could be enhanced through prayer. In other words, if people pray hard enough for something, the laws of nature will help them realize their dreams. Opportunity will present itself in the form of synchronicity.

Mitsuko freely shared her ideas with participants of the three-month workshop. It was the 1990s, and change was afoot in Japan. The economy was souring after a brief period of explosive growth, and now that the bubble had burst, Mitsuko watched as men her age at the trading firm were laid off or forced into early retirement. Women, generally paid less, weren't pushed out as quickly, but still, it was clear to Mitsuko that the age of lifetime employment had come and gone, and her job at the trading firm may go someday, too. What would she do if she were fired? She pondered this for several months, but in the back of her mind, she knew the answer: she would become an acupuncturist.

Yoga taught Mitsuko that the human body has several chakras which serve as pathways for energy; they are aligned with the body's major nerve centers. Mitsuko liked the idea of taking care of people, especially the elderly, perhaps because of her time nursing her mother. She opened herself to these ideas and found that one serendipitous event would lead to another. Soon, at the age of forty-seven, she was enrolled in an acupuncture school. She was still working at the trading firm, so she joined the three-year night course, which held classes every weeknight from six to nine-fifteen.

Most of Mitsuko's classmates were very young. Some were in their late teens, just out of high school; others were in their late twenties — they had typically worked elsewhere and slowly found their way to acupuncture. But Mitsuko never felt out of place in this setting. The energy of these thirty young students invigorated her. Plus, there was another factor: she was in love with Kenichiro, a classmate in his thirties. She and Kenichiro would go to Denny's after class, sitting quietly and studying until midnight. Mitsuko would sometimes bake him cookies, and he occasionally asked if he could borrow her notes to catch up on studying. But their relationship never progressed. Mitsuko told him once that she thought of him as much more than a friend. Kenichiro said he appreciated her feelings, but he gradually moved away from her without offering an explanation. To Mitsuko, the message was loud and clear.

Mitsuko moved on from Kenichiro and redoubled her studies. She loved this course, especially learning about the human anatomy. Despite her rugged schedule — working during the day, studying at night — she remained full of energy on most days. The more she learned about the human body, the stronger her fascination became. The thing that fascinated her the most was the dissection of a human body, which the whole class watched. It may sound odd, but Mitsuko found the experience pleasant — she was mesmerized by the beauty of the muscles, the internal organs and the entire structure of the body. The human body seemed like a work of art.

Mitsuko passed the national acupuncture test in one try and became a licensed therapist. A month after graduating, she left her job with the trading firm, opened a clinic and began her practice. During the first few months, she worked seven days a week, not wanting to let a single client slip through her grasp. Business grew through word of mouth, and within a year, she was breaking even.

In her second year of business, she had more time to herself. She learned how to create and operate a website, and in the process, became hooked on the Internet. By now, it was 2000, and though Internet dating was far from popular in Japan, Mitsuko used her handle, kirara-chan, named for her favorite anime character, to post messages on Internet sites. Soon she was meeting people online and setting up dates with them.

She met her first blind date at a cafe. She was nervous, but he turned out to be a gentleman, and she felt that online dating wasn't as dangerous as many people said. She had other dates via the Net – some would turn and leave as soon as they saw how old she was; others would become her clients; and still others became friends she would have lunch or dinner with. The men ranged in age from their thirties to their sixties.

She met Yukio over the Net because he was looking for an acupuncurist to help alleviate his chronic back pain. He was a computer engineer and spent long hours in front of the screen. He was thirty-eight, and Mitsuko was fifty-two, although she kept her age a secret for quite a while.

Yukio was a well-behaved client; he was very polite and quiet. In fact, he was so quiet that Mitsuko was never sure if her treatment was working on him. He rarely told her if it hurt or felt good. But he would let out a small, almost imperceptible groan or twitch a little when she hit the right spot. Yukio kept returning, so Mitsuko eventually told herself that the treatment must be doing some good.

After several sessions, Yukio asked Mitsuko out. She could tell that he was mustering up a lot of courage to ask her — he had waited until the last possible minute, with his hand on the doorknob, and she noticed that he was shaking when he turned to her to see if she could possibly ... make herself available ... for a date.

Sure, Mitsuko said, she would love to. He smiled in return. The following week, he took her bowling. The next date, they went to Chinatown. And after several dates, they kissed. By then, the two of them were spending every Sunday together, even though Sunday had been a busy day for her business. Several dates later, Yukio and Mitsuko took the next step.

They made love for the first time at her clinic. Yukio promised to be gentle, and he was. For a long time after that, he held her tight against his chest and told her he loved her. But all Mistuko could do was reflect on everything she had heard and read about reaching a state of ecstasy and orgasm. She didn't feel anything like that. Perhaps Yukio is not a very skilled lover, she thought. But she knew better than to bring this topic up.

Despite Mitsuko's sexual frustrations, their relationship started out smoothly. Yukio seemed quite content with her. He was skinny and she was plump, but he told her that he loved cuddling with a chubby woman with big breasts. He preferred that to a slender woman, he said. Yukio loved to cuddle and spoon, and the two of them grew quite close physically. Less than a half year after they started dating, they decided to get married.

Her friends and family seemed truly surprised when she told them. Some joked that she was robbing the cradle by marrying a thirty-eight-year-old guy who had never been married. Friends asked how she finally found her man. Mitsuko quietly soaked up all the attention. Her life has not been bad at all, she remembers thinking.

Yukio suggested that they keep the ceremony simple, considering their age, and only invite a few family members. Mitsuko concurred, although she wondered to herself why age should have anything to do with the size of a wedding. The wedding took place in a Shinto shrine, and Mitsuko wore a wedding kimono, called a *shiromuku*, fulfilling a childhood dream. She felt a lump in her throat when an elderly aunt, her eyes aglitter, whispered, "How I wish your mother could have seen how beautiful you are."

Everything went smoothly until the time for the group photos. The photographer asked people to pose in front of a paper screen used only at fortuitous occasions like weddings. Mitsuko naturally stood at the center with Yukio, and other people slowly figured out where to stand in relation to them. Yukio's mother stood next to him because she was the most important guest of all now that his father had died. Mitsuko's favorite aunt stood next to her. The best man and bridesmaid stood to either side, and the rest of the group bowed and offered each other advantageous positions closer to the center until everyone had settled into the group. Just then, Yukio's mother called the ten-year-old daughter of Yukio's younger sister. "Come here, Rina-chan," she said.

"Yes, grandma?"

"Rina-chan, you stand in the middle."

Rina was wearing a white dress with red flowers on it and matching ribbons around her pigtails. She looked at Mitsuko, tilting her head a bit, and asked, "Here?" as she pointed to the space between the newlyweds. Without waiting for an answer, Rina zoomed in between them and took her position. Nobody said a thing.

Mitsuko felt slightly offended. This was her wedding after all; why should a child of her sister-in-law come between the bride and groom? Does it look like this is Mitsuko's kid, like she is marrying a younger man who will now be the father to her ten-year-old daughter? Rina was a charming little girl; it wasn't her fault. But Mitsuko couldn't help but feel bitterness toward Kazue, her new mother-in-law. It was clear that Kazue did not approve of her son marrying a woman fifteen years older than him and just twelve years younger than his mother.

Ever since her husband passed away, Kazue had been living with Yukio. His sister had married quite young and had her own family, so Kazue and Yukio were left with each other. Kazue was never openly rude to Mitsuko, but Mitsuko felt subtle pressure and got the distinct feeling that Kazue did not approve of her son's choice for a bride.

Was Kazue bitter because her son was going to have a childless marriage? Whatever the matter, Mitsuko determined that she was not going to let the Rina episode ruin her wedding day.

But Rina was like an omen, standing there between her and Yukio. Or was she? Was she reading too much into this? She was a happy bride, full of hope. Push those anxious thoughts aside, Mitsuko thought. Later, when she finally saw the group photo, she thought that it didn't look bad at all. Everyone seemed quite happy, even Mitsuko.

The new bride felt confident about her future. Her husband had a good understanding of how important her acupuncture business was to her, so he wouldn't interfere with her career. But their wedding and subsequent newlywed days came at a very busy time for Mitsuko, who was launching her health-care-management business. She asked a friend to help her from time to time just to keep pace. But as much as possible, she did all the work herself, knowing that her clients would be disappointed if they didn't receive their treatment from her.

After the wedding, Yukio moved in with Mitsuko since she already had a house. But his idea of moving was odd: he only brought two bags full of underwear, shirts and pants and two business suits. Yukio said that his mom's place was just two train stops away, so he could just swing by there if he needed anything, plus this way, they could save space. Mitsuko had silverware, china, a fully furnished house — so why drag all his belongings over and clutter up the place?

This made sense to Mitsuko. After all, he needed to stop in and check on his mother from time to time anyway. Mitsuko felt bad about leaving her all alone, so letting Yukio make frequent visits seemed like a way of showing Kazue some respect.

Mitsuko had always liked to cook, but now that she was running two businesses, there were days when she just couldn't make it home in time to prepare dinner. On some nights, both Mitsuko and Yukio would work until nine-thirty or ten at night. They still tried to eat together and would often go out to a neighborhood spot — there were so many nice restaurants around them, and Mitsuko enjoyed trying them out. But on other nights, they'd just grab dinner by themselves. Mitsuko saw nothing wrong with this.

Soon, however, she realized that things were a little trickier than she had thought.

Yukio had never lived on his own. He could take basic care of himself — tie his own shoes, bathe himself, brush his own teeth — but that was about it. He didn't know the first thing about cooking, doing the laundry, folding his clothes. He didn't even bring his dishes to the sink after eating. Kazue had always done all these things for him.

Kazue's doting was far from extraordinary. In fact, it was more like the norm. Many women her age devoted themselves to their husbands and sons, and more than a few became even more fixated on caring for their sons once their husbands had passed away. This seemed to be the case with Kazue.

Yukio was also going through a difficult adjustment. He was slowly finding out that his wife had no intention to dote on him as his mother had. He was not one to complain too quickly, so he kept his mouth shut, but slowly the tension began to surface.

Mitsuko likes to take care of people — that's why she entered this line of work. But she was uncomfortable being a surrogate mother to a grown man. She was simply too busy for that sort of thing. Yukio didn't confront her; instead, he showed his defiance passively. He began to sleep over more and more at his mother's house. After six months of marriage, he was "going home" to his mother's house straight from work and visiting Mitsuko a few times a week. As their first wedding anniversary approached, Yukio was living with his mother again. He visited Mitsuko less and less during the next six months, and finally all he did was send her messages demanding a divorce.

Mitsuko never provoked a fight with Yukio or Kazue. But she also was not ready to give up on him. She didn't want Kazue to win. Mitsuko talked with Yukio and promised him that things would get better after she got her businesses on track. But Yukio responded with anger. He accused her of talking him into a marriage that he didn't want in the first place. He said that she had "deceived him" by pretending she could be a "good wife" who could provide for him. She was just buying time to torture him by not signing the divorce papers. He would shout these arguments at her over the phone until, one day, she gave up and agreed to the divorce.

Two years after their wedding day, Mitsuko and Yukio were divorced. Mitsuko didn't even bother to change back to her maiden name — it was too much trouble after switching all her bank accounts, driver's license and other IDs. She told a handful of her friends about the divorce, but otherwise, she went on with life as usual.

Mitsuko started taking classes to get certified as a health-care manager. She had to do some field work as well as study, and this kept her busy and happy. Her business grew as the years passed.

When Mitsuko reflects on her broken marriage, she feels like the script had already been written and she was just following it. With her business, she had no fear of failure. She knew, deep down, that she would be a success. Marriage was another story, but right now she has her infatuation with a certain Korean singer, and that makes her happy. She's quick to say she's not in love with him, not even in virtual love, but she does feel a karmic connection of some sort.

Mitsuko looks at her watch. It's ten-thirty. She has to leave for her clinic in a few minutes, but that's plenty of time to purchase that airline ticket to Seoul. She opens her browser, goes to Yahoo! Travel and searches through the package tours until she finds the right one. Next week, she will be in Seoul. The thought brings a smile. She says goodbye to Yuri as she leaves the office. Once she is out the door, she turns on her MP3 player and listens to his new album as she walks happily down the street.

THE MANNEQUIN

Ai Kusanagi, Office Administrator, 40

AS SOON AS AI closes the door, Masayuki picks her up and tosses her on the double bed, which occupies more than half the space of this hotel room. It's a decent hotel by Tokyo standards, which means it's pretty snug.

Masayuki is on top of Ai in seconds. With a smile, he tries to undress her. Ai quickly rolls on top of him, rips his jacket off, loosens his tie and unbuttons his shirt. He smiles and says, "Wow, wait a minute" — a half-hearted effort to slow their passion play.

Masayuki is enjoying every second of this, but Ai has other motives for stripping him down. One thing Ai really hates is leaving lipstick marks on Masayuki's clean, well-ironed shirts, which can be easily stained when Masayuki is in a hurry. The last thing she wants to do is to spend half an hour in the bathroom of the hotel, scrubbing a red mark off the collar of his shirt. That would really spoil the night.

There's no point explaining this to Masayuki. It's better just to rip his clothes off. Men are capable of being careless and silly when they are in love. And Ai wants to reward his love while minimizing his carelessness.

Masayuki is already in bed, naked. He is getting better at pleasing her. Ai never told him this, but Masayuki wasn't very smooth in bed when they started having sex. It was clear he hadn't experimented much — he needed training, and Ai trained him well. Masayuki proved a curious student willing to test the possibilities between them.

Masayuki is an industrious sort of guy, Ai says, and a thorough, passionate researcher. He has to have answers to his questions, and that has helped him learn what pleases Ai. Over time, he has found all of her pleasure zones, and this has made Ai deeply grateful.

Once they are done making love, Ai and Masayuki cuddle in each other's arms. This is their most peaceful moment. She forgets about everything that is bothering her, and her body melts into oblivion.

In the midst of a long, peaceful silence, Masayuki turns to her and asks, "Shall we go soon?"

Ai's heart goes numb and a sadness emerges from deep inside of her, spreading across her body. Masayuki is up and putting his pants on, but he seems to sense her sadness. He turns to her and kisses her softly. Behind him, Tokyo Tower stands illuminated against the night sky. Ai knows that Masayuki specifically requested this tenth-floor room because she once commented on how much she liked the view. This hotel is so much better than a tawdry love hotel with the trace of cigarette smoke reminding them of the couple who came before. And the location is quite convenient. Ai can catch an express train home from here, while Masayuki can also board his train, going in the opposite direction. They each have one-hour commutes ahead of them.

After leaving the hotel, they flag down a cab, and Masayuki directs the driver to the train station. Ai gets out first. There have been times in the past when Masayuki has paid her cab fare home from here. The sadness would overwhelm her on those nights, and she'd linger with him too long, missing the last train home. He'd always give her more than enough money to cover the cab fare. He's a very considerate man.

Ai taught Masayuki to use the sentence, "Shall we go soon?" In the first few years of their affair, he used to say, "We must go now." This would always get on her nerves, although she didn't say anything about it at first. Recently, however, she told him how it jars her and asked him to use the softer alternative. It helps keep some of the sadness at bay.

She told him: "I know we should go, but you don't have to say 'we must' to remind me. Could you please rephrase it with something like 'shall we?' I don't enjoy hearing the word 'now,' either, because I feel rushed. Perhaps, 'shall we go soon' would be better?"

Her intonation glides upward as she offers her alternative — Shall we go soon? — making the question mark emphatic. Masayuki took her suggestion right away and has been using the softer sentence ever since.

It didn't take long for Masayuki to express his affection toward Ai. "I love you, Ai. You are so beautiful," he told her shortly after they started going out.

Ai did not immediately return the compliment. In fact she held back. If she told him how she felt, he might feel burdened by it, she thought. But Masayuki has gradually convinced her that even though they are committing adultery, they should be honest with each other — verbally and spiritually. She could tell he was pleased when she started telling him, "I love you too."

Masayuki's dishonesty toward his wife was not something they would choose to talk about on their dates, but once in a while, the topic would emerge. Masayuki would say that while he loves Ai dearly, he also loves his wife. Ai recalls that he once told her: "We are a married couple. I have an obligation to support my wife. She's been supporting me throughout our life together, and she plays an important role — a role I appreciate. At some point in the past, she transformed from being my lover to my family member, and my love for her is similar to my love for my sister or my mother. I am fully aware that I am being dishonest and selfish by wanting you as you are, and I feel awkward about this. But I love you so much, and that's not a lie."

He explained to Ai that while he loves her, he will never consider divorce.

Having been married once herself, Ai understands his determination to protect his family. She says that she appreciates him for being so honest and considerate. He tells Ai how he loves his wife, although not in the same way that he loves Ai, and Ai accepts his feelings and loves him nonetheless. It is not easy — the truth hurts — but Ai says she would have dumped him a long time ago if he were the type to feed her cheap lines about how he doesn't love his wife and how Ai was the one and only.

Ai is sure Masayuki knows she's too smart to believe in cheap lines. Masayuki respects her and appreciates her strength, or at least she believes this to be so. That's why he can tell her the truth, Ai says. Masayuki is not a very verbal person, but he often apologizes for putting her in this difficult position. He reminds her that he deeply appreciates her love. Sometimes even his gestures — the way he moves around her — remind her of how much he cares.

Ai says Masayuki is always sincere with her. They are drawn together by mutual respect, not just animal magnetism, she says, although their physical attraction for each other is an integral part of their relationship.

By the same token, Ai can tell that Masayuki is passionately in love with her. Three years have passed since they started going out, but Masayuki seems head over heels for her still. He doesn't get mad if she complains about something — although she tries not to for her own peace of mind. Ai likes to think of herself as a giving person, someone who can soak up the bad to help those she loves. The more difficult, the better. Perhaps she is mildly masochistic, at least in a psychological sense.

At times she finds herself wishing his wife didn't exist. She doesn't want to share Masayuki. But then that thought quickly evaporates, in part because Ai can't picture her rival. She's never seen a photo of Masayuki's wife — all she knows is that she is a year younger than his wife and not quite as tall.

When Ai imagines Masayuki's wife, she's a mannequin without a face. She can't picture the style of clothes this woman likes — her image is devoid of personality. She's a mannequin, and Ai can't muster up enough anger to hate a mannequin. Ai is curious about Masayuki's wife, but her sensible side tells her it's better not to know.

Ai and Masayuki love each other, but Ai also knows that their relationship will evaporate into the ether as soon as she gets to know his wife. Ai knows her actions are immoral, but her guilt stays in check as long as she is cheating on a mannequin. If Ai saw Masayuki and his wife walking down the street, side by side ... well, that's the moment when Ai would say goodbye. This is what is called *kejime*: knowing where to draw the line.

❁

AI AND MASAYUKI worked at the same company when they started going out. It was innocent at first — nothing physical happened for the first two years. Ai was in charge of office administration in the trading department, which Masayuki ran. Ai was there before him, so when he arrived, she taught him the day-to-day details, including the good local lunch spots.

Masayuki is tall, good-looking and successful. But Ai had no sexual attraction toward him at first — none whatsoever. He was married, so she didn't even consider dating him. Masayuki, however, was mistaking Ai's friendly nature as a sign of her interest, as he confessed to her later.

Soon after Masayuki joined the company, they started having lunch together. It was just lunch for Ai, but Masayuki later confessed that he was already finding her attractive. They often talked about what was going on in the department. Other times, Ai talked about her sons, and their involvement in soccer. Although Masayuki was a soccer fan, he was sometimes perplexed about her lengthy descriptions of her sons' soccer games. At the same time, Masayuki started to feel deep admiration toward Ai for working full time while being such a loving mother. Ai took care of every detail of the department, gave her full attention to everybody on his floor and yet showed no indication of unhappiness or frustration about raising her sons alone. In fact, it took Masayuki a long time to realize that Ai was a single mother.

His admiration toward her continued to grow. Ai sat close to his desk, and Masayuki soon found himself glancing at her more than necessary. He just couldn't help but look at her. When he got a glance at her legs underneath the desk, he would blush.

He told himself to get a grip — I'm her boss. Plus, I'm married. Forget about her.

Ai was friendly to everybody, but Masayuki felt special in her eyes. One day during lunch, Ai was talking about her sons as usual, when she turned to him, looked him in the eye and said, "I think you will become a good father." Masayuki blushed. Was she talking about being a father to her sons?

Ai found all this out later, of course. At the time, she swears she had no idea how much she had agitated Masayuki's imagination. They were friends, but nothing more. Masayuki was a considerate boss. He was well liked too. He was sharp, unafraid of making quick decisions, and she couldn't imagine how his emotions roiled for her just below the surface.

This went on for two years — Masayuki lusting after Ai in his heart, but remaining boyish and platonic on the surface. Meanwhile, Masayuki's responsibilities at work grew. He was flying all over the world and was interviewing candidates for vacant positions in the department well after six PM when he was in town. He had other things on his mind as well: his mother, who lived on the southern island of Kyushu, was not well. He would fly to Kyushu almost every weekend to be with her. Ai watched and worried about him.

One night after work, Masayuki was invited to a casual party with his colleagues. He was exhausted, but he decided to make an appearance all the same. He noticed Ai as soon as he walked into the bar, and told her later that a feeling of relief swept over him.

During the party, Masayuki tried to grab Ai's attention, but his efforts were clumsy. Frustrated, he kept drinking until he was pretty drunk. As everyone headed home, Ai went to the restroom. When she came out, he was waiting for her. Shall we have another beer? he asked.

Masayuki later told her he was scared she would turn him

down. He is a calculating guy, and this was a risky move. She could have easily rebuffed him and told him to go home and get some sleep. Even worse, if she interpreted his request the wrong way, he could be brought up on sexual harassment charges. After all, he was a married man and her boss. But he just couldn't stop himself — his longing for her had grown into an obsession on this night, and he had to act. Stress and alcohol fueled his courage, but that wasn't the whole reason he waited for her. This had been building in him for two years — he could no longer deny his attraction to her.

To Masayuki's surprise, Ai paused for a moment and replied, "Sure." Ai says she wanted to support him — he was exhausted. She felt something akin to maternal love kick in, something like deep compassion.

They hailed a cab, and once inside the back seat, Masayuki squeezed her hand and embraced her. To Ai, it felt more like a boy clinging to his mother than a man trying to have an affair. She immediately sensed that she was not in the hands of a playboy.

In the cab, he kept shaking his head in disbelief and muttering about what a bad situation they were in. "This isn't good," he kept saying. He was obviously drunk.

"It's OK. Please don't worry," Ai said. "Just calm down, please."

The cab dropped them off at a beer hall. Masayuki held her close. Then his cellphone rang. He answered. Ai could tell it was his wife. He quickly ended the conversation, started shaking his head again, but he continued to hold her close.

As they left the beer hall, Masayuki invited her to a hotel. Ai knew this was coming, and she knew her answer would be yes. In the hotel, Masayuki was too drunk to perform. He lay on top of Ai, staring at her, muttering over and over (at least one hundred times, Ai recalls), "You are so beautiful."

❁

THE NEXT DAY, Masayuki invited Ai to lunch. After a few awkward minutes, Masayuki began, "About yesterday ..."

Ai interrupted before he could continue. "Let me speak first. I don't mind at all if you say, 'Let's pretend it never happened.' I understand your position and where you're coming from." She felt sincere as she said this.

Masayuki listened attentively, reflected for a moment and finally replied: "I'm not here to tell you 'let's forget about it.' I might have been drunk, but my feelings for you are genuine. I know I am selfish to say this, but I would like to see you again. I don't know when I can see you next time, maybe two months or three months from now, but I don't want this to end because I like you a lot."

Ai wasn't sure about her own feelings at that point. She liked Masayuki also — that was for sure — and she didn't want to break his heart, so she agreed to have a date with him. That date occurred two weeks later; they had another date two weeks after that. They continued to have lunch together and began emailing back and forth almost every day.

Ai and Masayuki continued to see each other, careful not to let their co-workers in on their secret. They made time once or twice a month, which was all they could manage with their busy schedules and their need to be discreet. But slowly, as their happiness increased when they were together, they started longing to see each other more.

At the same time, Masayuki remained tight-lipped about his wife. Masayuki had an unwritten code he lived by where he wouldn't bring his wife to social functions unless it was absolutely necessary. When both Ai and Masayuki were invited to a wedding or party or they had to attend a funeral, one or the other would come up with an excuse not to attend. Both were worried that Masayuki's wife would insist on attending, too.

When one of Masayuki's subordinates got married, Ai made an excuse. Back at work after the wedding, co-workers passed around photographs. Ai was curious, but she didn't look at them for fear of finding Masayuki's wife in one of them.

Only once did Masayuki offer anything about his wife. "She wants a child, but she hasn't gotten pregnant." There was a pause.

"As a mother, I know how important that is for her," Ai finally responded.

"That's why I respect you so much," Masayuki told her. "You are such a caring mother, and you work full time to support your kids."

He paused. Then he began telling Ai about his wife. Masayuki said that a few years after they were married, his wife stopped having sex with him. This was long before he met Ai, he assured her. He didn't offer any details or explain the sexual falling out, but Ai believed him. She had heard talk of sexless marriages, of men who say they love their wives like sisters or mothers but can no longer see them as objects of sexual desire.

Masayuki said he didn't dwell on the lack of sex until she said she wanted a baby. They began trying, but without success. They turned to fertility treatments as a last hope.

Masayuki also told Ai that his wife had had an abortion in the past, when she was still in college. "We were young. I didn't want to quit school to support a family then, so I asked her to have an abortion and she agreed. I married her soon after I graduated."

He didn't say that her infertility was linked to the abortion. He simply said that if he was going to give her a child, they needed to act now.

Masayuki's wife was in her late thirties, desperate for a baby.

Ai thought of her own son Ken. He was already a teenager, a good kid, but going through a difficult stage. He was a star athlete, and had been good at sports since a very young age. He played soccer on his junior high team and was looked up to by others because he was so good. In fact, he was good enough to get a full-ride at a prestigious high school next spring. He would get free room and board. Ai would miss Ken. She was very proud of him.

Ken was not a studious boy, however. And lately, there had been problems. Because Ai worked late, Ken and his little brother, Sei, ate dinner at her parents' condo, on the fifth floor of their building. Ai had bought a condo in her parents' building after her divorce. Ai's mother was a happy homemaker, and she readily offered to make dinner for the kids every weeknight but Thursday, when she had an ikebana class.

When Ai would get home from work, the boys were usually still up, so they had time to chat. When she worked very late, they were supposed to go to bed by eleven.

One night, Ai returned home to find a pair of high heels in her entranceway. She felt her heart start to pound. She checked Sei's bedroom first. He was sound asleep. Then she took a deep breath and knocked on Ken's door. "Can you please come out of your room?"

"What do you want?"

"Please come out for a second."

Ken swung open his door. He looked down at her — Ai was not short, but Ken was about six feet, at least a head taller than his mother. He wore pajama bottoms but no top.

"I know she is here again. Please tell her to go home now. You have school tomorrow."

It was almost eleven-thirty.

"Shut up! What is it your business?"

"It is my business. You agreed last time that you wouldn't

bring her here when Sei is around because it's a bad influence on him."

"Sei was already asleep," Ken protested.

"Fine. I believe you. But it's still my responsibility to supervise you because you're still a minor. It's getting late; please tell her to go home."

Ai closed the living room door behind her to give them some privacy. She heard Ken kicking the wall, cursing. Then she heard the girl gather up her stuff and leave. Good, Ai thought, at least she left of her own will.

The girl was two years older than Ken. Ai sensed that she was taking the initiative on these late-night rendezvous. Ai was shocked to learn that her fourteen-year-old boy was already involved in a physical relationship, but she told him as calmly as she could about condoms and the precautions he needed to take. After that talk, she found used condoms in his wastebasket. Her heart would pound as she pulled the sperm-filled condoms out of her son's trash.

Ai felt it was her responsibility to let the mother of the girl know about all this. The family lived upstairs, and Ai knew her from PTA meetings. Ai was expecting to be criticized for being too lenient with her son, but the mother said, "I'm glad it's your son. Ken-chan is a good boy. She could have ended up with a worthless kid."

Ai insisted that the children still needed supervision. The mother replied, "I have no control over her anymore, but thanks for letting me know. I will tell her to be careful."

❀

MASAYUKI WAS silent. Ai felt weird knowing that the man she was having an affair with was trying to make his wife pregnant, while at home, Ai was doing everything she could to keep Ken from getting someone pregnant. Would Ai become a grandmother before Masayuki became a father?

Ai let out a sigh. "As I said, I'm a mother. I know how important that is to your wife. When the stork arrives, I will leave you. Children must come first, whether they're yours or mine."

Masayuki was quiet for a while. "I'm sorry Ai. I will not stop you from finding a husband. Obviously, I have no right to stop you. You deserve a man who can take good care of you, although I will be desperately jealous when that does happen."

Ai was jealous herself from time to time. Despite Masayuki's reluctance to talk much about his marriage, Ai gradually began to piece together a picture of them in her mind. She was in charge of office administration, so she was privy to sick-leave requests, vacations and other personal requests. She knew, for example, that Masayuki took a few days off to look into possibly purchasing a second house somewhere on the Izu Peninsula. She had been aware of him owning a condo in Tokyo, where he lived with his wife, but the second house was a mystery to her. Neither one mentioned it.

On another day, Masayuki's wife called to tell him she had cut herself in the kitchen. The wound was deep, and she was bleeding heavily, so she had to go to the hospital to get stitched up. Masayuki asked for permission to leave the office early to be by her side.

That was the night they were supposed to see each other. She figured their date was cancelled, but then later in the day, he returned to the office. Ai asked casually if his wife was OK. He gave her a pale smile and said, "Thank you." Ai insisted that he go home that night.

❁

TWO YEARS after Ai and Masayuki began seeing each other, he decided to take a job with another company. His colleagues were planning his farewell party when one of the bosses approached Ai and casually asked her to buy something as a farewell gift. "Perhaps something that both he and his wife can use," the boss said, "you know, because they're so close."

Ai was sure the boss had no idea about her and Masayuki. But still, his comments stung. Masayuki never asked Ai out on the weekends; it was clear he devoted his weekends to his wife. Perhaps they traveled to that second home that Masayuki had recently purchased. Ai wondered what they did there. Did they play tennis or golf together? Or stay inside and read? Perhaps they were making love in the hope of having a child.

Ai asked Masayuki what he wanted for a farewell gift. He gave her a boyish smile and said, "An iPod Nano." They secretly went shopping for it later. Ai told the boss that she had asked Masayuki what he wanted so as not to waste the money his colleagues had raised. "That was a good idea," said the boss.

❁

AI KNEW she couldn't blame Masayuki for everything. She had her share of guilt too.

Ai had slept with Jim, an African-American computer engineer in charge of the information technology on Masayuki's floor. Jim was the classic playboy: He had a much younger Japanese wife; he was funny, talkative and good-looking with a killer body thanks to his steady weight-lifting routine. Jim became friends with Ai over time, and even though she knew he was a playboy, he turned out to be a very good listener. Their time together was pleasant.

On their first date, after a few drinks, Jim embraced her openly on the street and kissed her. On their third date, she agreed to go to a hotel with him. They slept together several times, but Ai eventually lost interest and stopped seeing him. Ai never really was clear why she fell for Jim for that brief spell. Was she curious? Or just lonely?

After Masayuki had left the company, Ai decided to tell him about Jim. Jim liked to boast of his exploits with women, and though she knew Jim would keep their affair secret at the office, now that Masayuki was working at a different company, Ai worried that Jim would tell him. She imagined the worst: Jim telling Masayuki buddy to buddy about making her scream in bed.

Masayuki and Jim were acquaintances, not good friends, but the two men still had drinks once in awhile. What if Jim got drunk and decided to tell Masayuki about his exploits at the office?

Ai had been jealous since Masayuki left because one of the women in the office gave him a kiss on the cheek and told him how much she was going to miss him. This woman was married and very serious at work. Ai couldn't believe it. Masayuki laughed it off, but she could tell he enjoyed it.

Ai was also frustrated that Masayuki had planned to spend a month overseas with his wife. Her reasons for confessing to an affair with Jim were clouded by this growing jealousy, but still, she expected him to forgive her.

He did not.

When she told him while they were together in a hotel room, he lay speechless on the bed for a long time, staring at the ceiling. Finally, he spoke.

"Why him? That's too much. How could you have done this to me..." he murmured. Masayuki remained still for a long time after that, then finally said, "Maybe we should go home."

Masayuki had issues about the size of his penis. He's a tall, slim, handsome man, and Ai felt his size was just right — not too big, not too small, but Masayuki confessed that he didn't have much confidence in that department. Ai said she never dreamt that Jim being black could become such a big issue. For an average Japanese man, being compared to a well-built black guy was like being condemned to death, she concluded.

Ai apologized. She began to cry. "I'm very sorry. I really am. I was jealous about your holiday with your wife. I won't see you for a month."

Masayuki was quiet.

Ai could tell she was losing him for good. She kept talking: "Size is not an issue. Jim was so big that it hurt. You make me come all the time, but he didn't. Size isn't what women are after. We need love, not a big dick."

Masayuki did not look convinced. Ai told him she didn't want to leave him, but it was up to him. Perhaps he could think about it over his holiday. He was married, after all, and she was just lonely.

Masayuki finally said he had no right to keep her from seeing whomever she wanted. It was selfish of him to expect her not to.

A few days later, Masayuki and his wife left on their vacation. Two weeks into the trip, Ai received flowers and a letter from Masayuki. It was Valentine's Day. Masayuki must have arranged this before he left. "I'm sorry to leave you so lonely," he wrote. "I really wish we were together. I will try to email you as much as possible."

❀

NOW THAT MASAYUKI is working for a different company, Ai sees him less. His office is a few subway stops from hers, so lunch is out of the question. Ai sometimes tells him she misses seeing him in the office. His reply is that these different experiences will strengthen their relationship, make them closer.

Her friends sometimes ask her why she continues to see a married man. Ai, you look younger than your age, they say, and you could easily get remarried if you try. Why waste your time with someone else's husband?

Most of Ai's friends get upset when they talk about the affair. They see Masayuki as irresponsible, sneaky even. When these conversations occur, Ai feels as if they are talking about someone she's never met.

Ai is used to this kind of thing. People would badmouth her ex-husband, Joji, too, especially when their marriage fell apart ten years ago. They called him a loser.

Ai married Joji when she was twenty and just out of vocational school. Joji was thirty-five and had already been divorced once. He had two teenage kids who lived with his ex. Everyone told her she was too young, but Joji was her first love. He was a good husband, too. Ai became pregnant soon after they got married. She was a very young mother, and sometimes Ken's crying would confound her. She had no idea how to make him stop. Some nights, she would be on the verge of tears as her baby son wailed by her side. Joji would come home, pick Ken up, change his diaper and rock him in his arms. Ken would slowly nod off, and Joji would lay him in the crib. She could always count on him. And he treated her like a princess.

When Ai found out about the other woman, it was very hard for her to accept the fact that she was no longer his little princess. She was replaced by a younger woman, who was destined to walk in Ai's footsteps — marrying, bearing children, raising them, being Joji's little princess for a time.

Ai knew that Joji was a womanizer. But she also knew that their marriage was deteriorating before the twenty-year-old came on the scene. During the last five years of their ten-year marriage, Joji lost several jobs and began to rely on Ai's income.

Joji was a carefree man. When Ai complained about their financial situation, he brushed her worries aside, saying that love would help them through it. "Why worry?" he would say with a smile. Ai was in her late twenties at that time, a skilled office administrator, but the burden of working and raising a family was crushing her.

Late at night, when she was washing the dishes, Joji would say, "Why don't you come here and relax a bit? I'll do the dishes tomorrow." He would do them, too, and he would help with the laundry. But that wasn't what Ai wanted. She wanted him to get a job, not stay at home and do housework. This was eventually the thing that undid their marriage. She would confront him about his unemployment, and he would turn cold and say, "But I washed more dishes and changed more diapers." Ai knew her marriage was all but over.

Ai believes that is why he strayed from her. Ai rarely sees him anymore, but he keeps in touch with the children. It can be frustrating, Ai admits, that she has had to raise their children without even a hint of child support from him, but she doesn't hate Joji. When other women complain about their exes, calling them assholes or losers, Ai feels very distant from them. It's not in her to hate him.

The same goes for Masayuki. Ai can't imagine herself cursing at him or throwing things at him. Yes, she wishes they could be together. But she is not dependent on him, either psychologically or financially. She also can't imagine Masayuki moving in with her and her two sons. For Ai, her children come first. They anchor her. Falling in love is one thing and being a good mother is quite another. If her children want pork cutlet for dinner, then they get pork cutlet. She doesn't have to factor in her husband's wishes.

When Ai feels especially weak, she wishes Masayuki could

support her financially. But she wouldn't be happy as a full-time homemaker. She's not in love with her work, but she is proficient and confident. Joji's line — "I washed more dishes than you" — would be easier to take than a husband who says, "Look at how much money I've spent on you."

❁

WHEN AI got divorced, she felt a lot of pressure to remarry. But that idea and those pressures have evaporated. Ai still avoids the mall on the weekends — she doesn't like seeing all those happy couples shopping — but her children and her relationship with Masayuki keep her busy. Masayuki has been good about giving her advice on how boys need to be treated. But she also knows that she is nearing the end of her child-rearing days. What's next, she wonders. She has no idea.

Ai started taking flamenco lessons recently. She wanted to find something independent from her children. Her friends tell her she is already very independent, but Ai is not convinced. She has given so much energy and time to raising her two boys that her life is intertwined with theirs. But soon, she must stand on her own.

Flamenco is her first step toward independence, Ai says. And today is Wednesday, the day of her weekly lesson. After work, she will say goodbye to her colleagues, grab her bag with her flamenco shoes and fling open the door. ❁

THE SHINTO PRIEST'S WIFE

Shoko Omori, Housewife, 38

ALTHOUGH SHOKO'S HOUSE was in the middle of Tokyo, she would wake up in summer to the cries of cicadas and be lulled to sleep in autumn by the crickets. Shoko's husband, Masanobu Omori, was the chief priest of an historic Shinto shrine in the city. Shoko and her father-in-law, Masashi, managed all the shrine's festivities, and the family lived in a building on a corner of the vast shrine grounds.

Shoko was not particularly religious. When she and her siblings were growing up, their father, a college professor, and their mother, a full-time homemaker, took them to a shrine on New Year's, but that was about it. She never imagined in her wildest dreams that she'd be living this close to the gods. Shoko's major in college was business administration, and she held a job as a computer-systems engineer. Before she was married, the most she could say about the difference between Shinto and Buddhism was that shrines belonged to the Shinto faith and temples were Buddhist. She didn't have a clue about the proper offerings at a shrine, what sort of events were held or how a shrine made money.

Of course, the man she loved didn't just decide to become a Shinto priest one day. Masanobu came to it slowly, eventually agreeing to inherit the position from his father. When it was decided that he would take over, an announcement was made, Shoko and Masanobu were married and — just like that — she became the Shinto priest's wife.

Shoko says she actually believed her mother-in-law, Toshiko, when the woman told her, "A priest's wife does just what a typical housewife does."

❀

SHOKO AND MASANOBU rented an apartment for a few years after getting married, so she didn't really feel like a Shinto priest's wife in the early days of their marriage. When they moved into the corner building on the temple grounds with Masanobu's parents, Masanobu told her: "It's old, but at least it's spacious." There was no comparison, space-wise, with any of the apartments in the vicinity, and while they'd be living in the same building as his parents, he promised that they would remodel the place into a modern, two-generation home with separate entrances and kitchens. She was worried about getting along with her in-laws, but she kept telling herself that she was lucky to live in such a spacious environment.

"So this is what it's all about," she remembers thinking once she had given birth to their first son and the family had moved into the building on the shrine grounds.

The first thing that surprised her was how people she had never seen before knew who she was. She was the focus of attention among the locals. Soon after they moved in, Shoko went grocery shopping one day. When she returned home, Toshiko said, "So you bought eel today."

"How did you know that?"

"Tanaka-san from the neighborhood spotted you at the supermarket," came the reply.

Wherever she went, the neighbors made it their business to know what the priest's wife was up to. It wasn't that she had anything to hide, but she still remembers feeling pressured. "I can't do anything wrong here," she thought.

Another thing she learned is that the gods don't take vacations. Most of the shrine's activities were on weekends and holidays, so the family couldn't have a normal weekend. Around the New Year and during the season of seven-five-three festivities,[1] they were so busy that Shoko remembers feeling there was barely time to catch her breath. Masanobu didn't have to commute to work, and while it was reassuring having him around all the time, they had to receive guests morning, noon and night. The lack of privacy troubled her. She was surprised

1 7-5-3 celebrations, known as shichi-go-san (七五三), are held at Shinto shrines throughout Japan on or around November fifteenth. Boys and girls turning three that year, boys turning five and girls turning seven dress in formal wear (usually hakama for boys and kimono for girls, but sometimes Western-style suits and dresses as well) and go to the shrine to have their picture taken.

when people came in the middle of the night, rang the doorbell and asked to buy an amulet. They couldn't just act like typical storeowners and tell the customers to come back during business hours, and it was tough not to let her frustration show on her face. They had far more guests, phone calls and special occasions to deal with than the average Japanese family. In recent years, Shoko has become comfortable enough to allow herself a sarcastic comment or two when the family becomes busy preparing for a big event.

"Ah, I was tricked into doing this by *okasan*," she once said, referring to her mother-in-law.

Toshiko sniffled and said, "You're the fool for being tricked."

Toshiko wasn't entirely wrong, so Shoko couldn't fight back. Maybe that's why some people see me as a little off, Shoko thought. If you put a good spin on it, she was magnanimous, but put a bad spin on it and she seemed a little slow. Masanobu had said that someone slow like Shoko was just right for getting along with Toshiko, who promptly sized up a situation and didn't hesitate to make her pronouncements. "She's a nice person, but she has a terrible mouth," Shoko thought to herself.

The more Shoko thought about it, the more she felt that being a priest's wife was her mission in life — she was an obliging person who liked people.

After they had married, Shoko asked him, "Why did you want to marry me?"

"Do you remember Professor Ishihara?"

Masanobu and Shoko were classmates at university, and they were both in Professor Ishihara's class. The professor was a very punctual man, and he was known for showing up at the classroom about fifteen minutes before class started. Shoko would arrive after him, and whether Professor Ishihara looked at her or not, she would turn toward his desk and give a very polite bow.

"In that big of a class, when you weren't even late, you were the only one who would bow like that," he told her. "When I saw you do that, I thought, oh this woman might be just right for a priest's wife."

All Shoko remembers of that class is that no matter how hard she tried, she could never arrive more than ten minutes before class started. As she walked into the classroom, she would see Professor Ishihara standing there and get a sinking feeling. "Ah, he's already arrived."

❀

SHOKO AND MASANOBU met in a computer seminar at university. While Masanobu was from a family that had a long history of running Shinto shrines and he was in line to inherit the family business, his parents wanted him to have a normal university education to polish his skills and help him learn about society at large. This is how he ended up in a typical private university with Shoko. At the same time, both Shoko and Masanobu were seeing other people during their college years, and Shoko never thought that she'd end up married to him. In those days, the future Shinto priest was into punk rock. He had spiked hair, boots and metal decorations dangling from his belt that would clink together as he walked. He had a severe air about him and was, frankly, scary-looking. Masanobu was the student leader of the seminars and Shoko did the accounting.[1] During their work on the seminars, they were forced to communicate a lot, but he intimidated her, and she would avoid talking directly to

1 Most Japanese social groups, including college seminars, have a team leader, an accountant (to manage contributions for farewell gifts and the like) and a record keeper.

him by telling others to talk to him: "Please give this to Omori-san." "Please ask Omori-san about this." One of Shoko's male friends found this so amusing that he once brought Shoko to Masanobu and said to her, "Talk to him directly."

Masanobu was a self-reliant guy who liked to lead. Shoko's boyfriend Nobuyuki was the exact opposite — he liked to talk over every decision. During university, Masanobu wasn't even on Shoko's radar.

Nobuyuki was one year older than Shoko, but because he failed the entrance exam twice, he was in the class behind her at school. The first time she ever talked to Nobuyuki was in their tennis circle, in the spring of Shoko's sophomore year. A senior had called her and some others over and told them to hand out leaflets around campus so the circle could recruit some new members. While she was handing out the leaflets, she met Nobuyuki. Her friend had spotted him first and said, "Hey, he's your type, isn't he? Shall we go chat with him?" She grabbed Shoko's hand and led him to Nobuyuki. He was tall, dark and had an angular, well-built body. He handled himself like an actor, moving gracefully. Shoko fell for him right away. She was usually reserved in these situations, but she figured there was little chance he would talk to them anyway. With nothing to lose, she chatted with him and asked him to join their tennis circle: Nobuyuki was happy to oblige. A few months later, they were dating. And for the rest of her university days, Shoko was with Nobuyuki. When they were about to graduate, both parents were aware of the relationship, and Shoko figured they would soon be married.

Yet, during all their time together in college, their sex life consisted of making love several times when they had first started dating. Since then, for most of the five years they had been together, their relationship was largely platonic. One of

Nobuyuki's friends had gotten a woman pregnant, and there was talk that his family paid one million yen to end the relationship. "If that happened to us, you'd be the one to get hurt, so I can endure until we get married," Nobuyuki would tell her. Since then, he had never asked Shoko for sex. That was fine for Shoko at the time, too. "You might be surprised to hear this, but there weren't many women in the Economics Department and we didn't really talk about that sort of thing. I thought this was what was happening to everyone," Shoko said. But when she later told her friend about her relationship with Nobuyuki, she was surprised by the friend's response. "Shoko, you were really raised right," her friend said.

❀

AFTER GRADUATION, Shoko took a job as a systems engineer. "I didn't think too much about it; I just took the job," she says. Meanwhile, Masanobu had to go to a different university to continue graduate studies for the priesthood. But the students in the seminar that Masanobu and Shoko had run often got together for reunions and events, so the two saw a lot of each other. Often, Masanobu and Shoko were seated right next to each other. He would sometimes call her office and say, "Let's all get together for a drink and something to eat." Shoko was still seeing Nobuyuki and assumed they would eventually get married, but she thought to herself, "There's no harm in going out with classmates and having a meal before I get married." She didn't keep it a secret, either, telling Nobuyuki and her other friends that Masanobu had called to invite her to a meal with other classmates. In the beginning, she had nothing to be ashamed of, so she didn't hide the fact that he was calling her.

Masanobu had never actually hit on Shoko. About two years after they had graduated, a friend of Shoko's said to him, "You know, Shoko-chan has a boyfriend. Why do you keep asking her out?" Out of the blue, Masanobu said, "Because I plan to marry her." Shoko's friend burst out laughing. Shoko laughed too. "What? Is that some kind of joke?" But inside, she had to admit, it didn't feel bad. It was from this point on that Shoko started being interested in Masanobu.

Over time, Shoko started seeing Masanobu more often, but they were always with others. Shoko felt strongly that while she was seeing Nobuyuki, she wouldn't see Masanobu alone. But in those days, she and her friends were going over to Masanobu's place more and more. Without consulting her, the Omori family was starting to consider Shoko as a candidate for their son. One day, his mother, Toshiko, surprised Shoko by asking, "So do you think you want to come here as a bride?" Shoko saw Toshiko as a very strict woman at the time. All she could mutter in reply was, "Ah, I don't think so. I just couldn't handle the responsibility."

LOOKING BACK, it seems like a luxurious thing to worry about, but for about a year, Shoko went back and forth in her mind between Masanobu and Nobuyuki. Which one should she choose? During that year, she watched a TV program called "IF," which sketched out people's lives depending on the paths they could choose. "If they selected this path, their life would turn out this way, and if they selected the other path, their lives would change," she recalls. "The narrator would say, 'Well then, if it were your decision, which path would you choose?' I remember thinking that it was like the narrator was talking about me!"

If she just went with her feelings, she would have chosen Nobuyuki. He was the type of guy who would hold her hand and ask, "What shall we do? What do you want to do?" They always did things together and they could talk about anything, and being with him made her feel good. Another plus was that Shoko's father really liked Nobuyuki. Shoko had thought to herself that she might have a father complex — she was always her daddy's daughter, and when he was home from work on a weekday when she was a high school student, she remembers that she couldn't wait to get home and see him. He'd take her shopping and they'd cook together. Her dad would start drinking, and she enjoyed telling him in detail about goings-on at school. She had heard that adolescent girls went through a period of hating their fathers, but Shoko never experienced it. There were things she couldn't talk about with her mom that she would bring to dad. When she started dating Nobuyuki, she introduced her dad to him first. Her dad had once told her, "Shoko, I think Nobuyuki is right for you." Part of her agreed: maybe he is the guy for me.

Masanobu, on the other hand, was the type to pull Shoko along. She did feel comfortable with him, and while being the wife of a priest would be difficult, his job was secure. If she wanted a peaceful life after marriage — a life void of fears of bankruptcy or unemployment — maybe joining the Omori family was the right thing to do. Masanobu hadn't actually proposed to her yet, but when they met, he would say things like, "Are you going to break it off with him?" She had a feeling that he was serious about her. A male friend from her university seminar days who knew both Masanobu and Nobuyuki told her she'd be better off going with a guy like Masanobu. She'd listen to this advice and think to herself: "I wonder if I have a father complex. I want a strong person."

In the end, the deciding factor was the fact that Nobuyuki had a weak heart. Whenever he got an electrocardiograph test during his health check-up, he would be called back for a second test. They were still in their early or mid-twenties at this time. What would happen if he died young? This would overwhelm her with worry at times. "I loved him, so I worried about whether I could bear it if he died or whether I could raise a child alone. It was during these times that I started to realize that love and marriage were two different things."

When Shoko would mention the subject of breaking up to Nobuyuki, he would lie prostrate at her feet and beg her to reconsider. "Please don't break up with me! Marry me," he would say as he cried. Once, when he was drunk, he sat down in the middle of the street. Many times, on her way to work, she'd see Nobuyuki and his mother waiting for her. Nobuyuki's mother would approach her and cry, "Shoko-chan, don't break up with him. Marry my son." All Shoko could say in reply was "I'm sorry, but I'm on my way to the office. I must go to work, so please excuse me." When this sort of thing happened, she knew she couldn't marry this man. Compared to Nobuyuki's approach, Masanobu seemed downright confident and calm.

She did not make a point of telling Masanobu when she broke up with Nobuyuki, but the next time he asked her to dinner, she replied quickly — "Sure" — and he sensed that something had changed. Shoko had always asked who was coming with them, but this time she didn't.

"Did you break up with him?"

"Mmm hmm."

Masanobu didn't ask any more questions. When Shoko looks back on this exchange, she realizes that this is when their plans for marriage became official. Masanobu was a shy person; he never did propose to her formally. The closest he came to popping the question was once when they were singing at a karaoke bar. He told her, "Listen carefully," then sang, "Won't you be my wife?"

Shoko has to admit that her mother-in-law Toshiko's way with words swayed her decision to marry Masanobu. Shoko saw

Toshiko as "blunt and intimidating, but someone who wouldn't lie." So when Toshiko told her, "Being the wife of a priest is just the same as being a full-time housewife. You don't have to bother with the shrine itself. Just take care of your home," Shoko thought to herself, "OK, that makes sense. Perhaps I can do this."

Toshiko had more: "If you marry a typical salaried worker, you'd rarely have time together. But at the shrine, you're always together. Doesn't that sound nice?"

"Yeah," Shoko thought, "being together all the time does sound nice."

Looking back, Shoko says, "I suppose in normal circumstances, a person would figure out pretty quickly that what she was saying wasn't true. But I didn't understand. I thought, 'So I really don't have to do anything with the shrine, huh? Great. I can be a full-time homemaker like I've always wanted.'"

It wasn't until the day of her wedding that she started to get an inkling of the rich historical lineage of the Omori family. The go-between, a sometimes symbolic position at a Japanese wedding, was a chief priest from a famous shrine. The guest list was filled with Shinto priests, and many of the relatives in attendance were connected to shrines. Shoko felt like she had entered another world.

❀

THE COUPLE'S newlywed days started well. Just as Shoko was getting into her new role as a full-time homemaker and the two were really getting to know each other and enjoying each other's company, Shoko became pregnant. When she went to the doctor and found she was five weeks pregnant, Shoko had been married for half a year and was twenty-five years old. "I'm not ready to be a mother. I don't have the confidence," Shoko said to a friend of hers with a child. Shoko couldn't hold back the tears.

"What are you talking about?" her friend retorted. "You know children are lovable, don't you?"

"I do, but I'm still not ready. I'm not qualified," Shoko said, sobbing. She felt queasy and overcome with anxiety. It took Shoko two weeks to gather the courage to say to herself, "I'm ready to become a mother."

At her seven-week check-up, the newly determined Shoko was dealt unexpected sorrow.

"I am sorry, but you've suffered a miscarriage."

At first, she didn't believe the doctor. How could the life inside her be gone when she had felt no pain, saw no blood? In shock, she called Masanobu and reported, "They say the baby in my stomach is dead."

Masanobu was working at the university in those days and he couldn't come home right away. But when he came home that night, it was apparent that he had talked to people and did some research on the subject. "This happens sometimes," he told her. "There's nothing we can do, so let's let it go.

"But just in case," he added, "you should go to another hospital and get a checkup tomorrow."

The next day, Shoko went to another obstetrician at a different hospital. "This may sound harsh, but the lifeless embryo is nothing more than garbage in your stomach now. If you don't get it out of there, you'll cause your body harm," the doctor told her. "If you want to have children in the future, you should have this taken care of right away."

It was a small hospital. In the waiting room, several mothers clung to their newborn babies. "Look how big your baby has gotten!" one chirped to another. In the other room, Shoko was being treated for her miscarriage. Her mind raced. "Why did this happen? Did it die because I said I didn't want it?" She cried as the doctor helped her deliver the dead baby.

Shoko had their first child, a boy, two years later. Having already had a miscarriage, Shoko constantly faced the fear of having another one. She would get tense whenever she went in for check-ups, thinking, "Is it still alive?" A pediatrician friend of Masanobu's saw Shoko and told her, "No matter how much science advances, it can't replace the womb. Science can't raise a baby in the womb like a mother can. But if the baby is small at birth, we doctors can step in and save the child. If the newborn is at least five hundred grams, in this day and age, there's a chance that we can help. Don't worry so much. Have a big heart and live your life."

Thanks to this friend's introduction, Shoko started going to the obstetrics and gynecology department of a hospital attached to a certain university. But no matter how calm she seemed, she admitted later that she never quite got rid of that dread of losing another child.

She gladly left these feelings behind when she gave birth to a healthy son. But once he was born, the next struggle was raising him. Perhaps her computer background and her penchant for seeing things in black and white got in the way. She liked to go by the book, and she wasn't very flexible in her approach to child rearing. Whatever the reason, Shoko suddenly felt like she was lost in a foreign country with no map and no language skills. When the baby would cry for a spell, she'd feel a dark cloud above her. I've changed your diaper and breast-fed you. Why are you still crying? For quite a while, raising her one son took everything she had. She couldn't even imagine having another one.

Two years passed before she thought that maybe she could handle another child. It was right around this time that she became pregnant again. But this one led to another miscarriage.

The doctor told her, "Let it go. It's as if you were in a traffic accident. These days, one in ten, if not one in seven or eight women have a miscarriage. Change your emotions and wait for your next pregnancy. Give it a half year, and you can get pregnant again."

About six months later, she was pregnant once more. But once again, she had a miscarriage.

This time, it was a different doctor who informed her of the news, but she said the same thing as the previous doctor: "Let it go. It's as if you were in a traffic accident." Maybe doctors had gotten together and agreed this would be the stock phrase for a miscarriage. Shoko couldn't suppress her emotions. She broke down crying. "Maybe one in ten people get into traffic accidents, but this is my third miscarriage! In six months, I've miscarried twice! There has to be something wrong. Please figure it out."

Japanese medical regulations stipulate that a woman who has suffered three straight miscarriages is covered for a medical examination, but since Shoko had given birth normally in between her miscarriages, her insurance wouldn't cover a checkup, the doctor explained. "If you insist, I will oblige, but it may take a mental toll on you."

Shoko couldn't bear repeating these miscarriages. She'd rather face the bad news. She asked the doctor to examine her.

As a result, she was told that she suffered from an autoimmune disease known as APS, or antiphospholipid antibody syndrome. When Shoko became pregnant, the doctor explained, the body treated the embryo like a foreign object and wouldn't send blood to it, making miscarriages or premature births likely. One treatment for this condition is to take a small amount of aspirin to improve circulation. This treatment is also used on people at risk of apoplexy. However, an injury can cause hemorrhaging and even loss of life. You must be cautious with injuries and avoid having dental work done on your teeth, the doctor added. Also, because a person's circulation improves on this treatment, there is a danger of massive bleeding during childbirth, so women should stop taking the dosage before delivering the child.

Shoko had been prone to edema when she was pregnant with her son and was prescribed a Chinese medicine before she gave birth. It might have been a coincidence, the physician said, but that medicine also helped in circulation and may have been the reason she was able to safely give birth to her son. If Shoko was worried about the aspirin, she could also prescribe some of the Chinese medicine.

The origin of the APS disease was unclear, the doctor reported. It's considered an intractable disease, and Shoko may find it affecting her as she aged. Shoko paid little heed to the doctor's words at this point. She just kept thinking that if she could have another child, then she should do it soon.

Given this background, Shoko was delighted that, at the age of thirty-two, she could give birth to their first daughter. She held the newborn to her chest for hours. "She was cute like a little puppy or kitten. Without thinking, I said, 'Doctor, can I give birth to one more?' When she replied, 'Sure. But give yourself half a year,' I really felt happy."

"You are psychologically prepared for her this time around," her mother-in-law Toshiko told her later.The three miscarriages had left her fearful of never having another child. Then she would put even greater pressure on herself by thinking about how she needed to raise their one son just right. There was more: even in the twenty-first century, the prevailing image of shrine families is that they had lots of children. Before Shoko had conceived the second child, an old man they knew well would call out to her, "We're still waiting for the next child!" He was trying to be nice, so she'd turn it into a joke, saying, "You wait. I'm going to make a lot!" But secretly she would feel a pang of desire as she heard those words again and again. She fought the pressure and raised her son, the stress building below the surface.

When her daughter was born, she felt love she hadn't felt

before. When her son would crawl at a department store, all she could think of was the dirt and grime. She would reach for an antibacterial wet tissue and wipe him off, all the time feeling anxious. When her daughter did the same thing, Shoko found herself smiling and saying, "What a good crawler you are!" Her daughter was also healthier than her son, who would easily break out in fevers when younger. The baby girl didn't get fevers and she held her food down. They rarely had to go to the hospital.

HOWEVER, SHOKO'S daughter finally did break out in a fever as she approached her first birthday. Shoko took her to her family doctor just in case. Luckily, it was only a cold. Before she could leave, the doctor turned to her and said, "It's about time for you to have that womb cancer test, isn't it?" Shoko thought that she wasn't due to have this test just yet, but since she was already at the doctor's office, she agreed to have it done right there.

A few days later, the doctor called. "Could you and your husband find time to drop by my office?"

Shoko thought there was something wrong with Masanobu's father, who lived with them and saw the same doctor. But when she and Masanobu arrived at the doctor's office, he looked at her and said, "Does your stomach hurt? Do you feel sick?"

He explained that the results of the womb cancer test were troubling, but he wanted Shoko to have another exam at a larger hospital as soon as possible.

Shoko was shocked. She had gone to the doctor because of her daughter's fever, and she came away with this? Panicked, she went to another hospital for a test and was told they had found some "aberrant material" in her womb. However, it was not cancerous and there was no need for surgery. Shoko was to come back in three months for more tests. It was another year before she was told she could become pregnant again. During this year, Shoko had decided that she wanted a third child. If she contracted uterine cancer, she wouldn't be able to have another baby. One more child, she thought. Then they can have my uterus. This is my last chance to give birth.

When she gave birth to their second daughter, she felt even more relief than when her first daughter was born. People often say that while your own children can be difficult, there's nothing cuter than a grandchild. Shoko's feelings for her second daughter were similar to how a new grandparent must feel. Shoko felt that she had learned a love that was more transcendent and objective than the love she felt for her first son and daughter.

"When you hear that someone has three children, it sounds like they had no problem delivering them," Shoko says. "But in my case, each pregnancy posed different problems that I had to overcome. I understand with my whole body how hard it is to have a safe and healthy birth. Without all this, I might have thought it was simple to have and raise healthy kids. The gods were testing my easygoing nature, I believe."

Shoko's second daughter has turned three and will start preschool in the fall. Shoko is constantly busy, raising three kids ages ten, six and three, and tending to the work around the shrine, but the thing that makes her most happy is that all three children are healthy.

❀

MASANOBU PLAYED a big role in Shoko's ability to overcome all the obstacles before her. He was quick to praise her, and though he didn't show much affection outwardly, he told her, "A man shows his feelings through action. Watch what I do and you'll know how I feel." He had an old-fashioned temperament like her father, Shoko thought. You could rely on him.

Shoko understood the true depth of Masanobu's thoughtfulness from about the time she was six weeks away from delivering their second daughter. Shoko was waxing the floor, working around her bulging belly, when Toshiko peeked her head in the door and said, "How are you feeling? You don't have to wax the floor today. Come have a cup of tea."

Shoko and Masanobu lived on the second floor, and Toshiko and her husband lived on the first. Toshiko would pop in like this to invite Shoko for tea every so often. This time, Shoko nonchalantly replied, "OK," and waddled down the stairs, plopping herself on a mat in Toshiko's living room with a sigh of "Yoissho!" Recently, when Shoko moved around even a little bit, her body felt heavy and tired, but she attributed this to evidence that the baby was growing. Right at this moment, the baby started kicking.

When Shoko looked up, she realized that Masanobu was sitting next to his mother. He doesn't take tea with us at this hour, she thought, and then she noticed an oxygen tank in the corner of the room.

"What's with the oxygen tank?" Shoko asked. Masanobu ignored her question: "Shoko, your father has left us."

"Left us? Where did he go?"

"Remember when the police came here late at night? Actually, they were searching for your father."

She remembered: on a night last week, the police came several times and talked to her husband and father-in-law. But the Omori family had a lot of visitors, and the police often acted as guards during celebrations and the New Year holidays, so a visit from the police wasn't particularly unusual. Last week when they came, Masanobu said, "You go ahead and get some sleep." She remembers thinking that he was worried about her and wanted her to rest, and she didn't even think about what the police were talking about.

"What do you mean he's gone? Why do the police have to look for him?" Shoko asked with fear in her voice. Masanobu explained that about two weeks ago, her father had not returned home after going out. Her father was a diabetic, and her mother worried that he may have fallen after his blood sugar level dropped, so she asked the police to help her find him. When someone found his body, the authorities took him to a nearby hospital, but he was already dead. He didn't have any identification on him, so the hospital called the local police. It took a long while for Masanobu to find him because the police didn't find any bruises or injuries and decided not to investigate.

"We weren't sure when to tell you, considering that you are carrying a baby, so we decided to be silent until things became clear," Masanobu said. "Actually, tonight is the wake."

Shoko was so shocked no words came to her. "Breathe into this," her husband said as he brought forth the oxygen tank. Desperate, she hung onto his arm and put the mouthpiece over her mouth, breathing in the oxygen. Her tears flowed down her cheeks.

❁

LEANING ON her husband, Shoko attended the wake and then the funeral. As people came up and offered condolences, all she could do was bow her head and say, "Thank you." She couldn't even feel the loss of her father. Unable to wail with her young son beside her, Shoko absent-mindedly made her way through the wake.

Shoko later found out the rest of the story: when Shoko's father went missing, Masanobu and his father went out every night searching for him. They ascertained where he last visited, appealed to the local police and visited all the hospitals in the vicinity. At the same time, they visited Shoko's doctor and discussed when to tell her the bad news. She was taking small doses of aspirin to fight her disease and give the embryo a chance to grow, and yet her due date was still two months away. The doctor told Masanobu and his father that the baby might not make it if Shoko went into labor now and, for the baby's sake, they should wait as long as possible to break the news to her. When the body was found and the dates for the wake and the funeral were set, Masanobu went to the doctor and told him, "If she gives birth and her father doesn't come to visit, she'll be shocked. I'd like her to attend the funeral if at all possible."

The doctor said he would have his staff ready in case she went into labor. He gave Masanobu the oxygen tank.

During the searches and after the body was found, Shoko never had an inkling that anything was wrong. Masanobu pretended that everything was normal when he was with her.

Masanobu wasn't the only one anxious about Shoko's health. Once the funeral was over, Masanobu took her home, telling her she'd sleep better if she didn't go to her parents' house right away. But she was filled with emotion and couldn't sleep. She kept waking up and took frequent trips to the toilet throughout the night. Afterwards, she found out that her mother-in-law was so worried that Shoko was going to try to kill herself that she stayed awake all night without napping.

"You are such a trouble-maker," Toshiko told her with a laugh well after the fact. "I was so worried about you, I couldn't sleep."

Through her father's death, Shoko found that while the Omori family wasn't one to heap praise on her, they really cared for her.

Supported by the warmth of her family, Shoko delivered a healthy baby girl on her original due date. When the child was born, Shoko took the little girl in her arms and began to cry. *My loving, protective family made sure this child would make it into the world,* Shoko thought, *and my father is probably looking after us from heaven.*

❀

THE OMORI family's love for each other wasn't created in one night. In the beginning of her marriage, Shoko often cried by herself at the severe treatment she received from her mother-in-law. "I'm proud of the way I raised Masanobu's two elder sisters," Toshiko would say. The two were good at everything, and easy-going Shoko became a bride without knowing anything about shrine life. Whatever Shoko did, she never got it quite right. She had no other choice but to go to Toshiko and ask her what to do. What should she prepare for the seven-five-three celebrations? When someone is awarded the governor's medal, what sort of gift should be given? How should the shrine be cleaned? There was so much she didn't know …

Toshiko must have been disappointed that she was stuck with this do-nothing daughter-in-law. Shoko felt desperate in just about everything she did, and as she failed, she felt miserable, but Toshiko's constant comments were especially tough to take. She would usually endure them without a reply, but every once in a while she would break down in tears in front of Toshiko, her father-in-law and Masanobu.

"I'm trying my best," she would plead.

During her breakdowns, Masanobu would pretend not to notice, quietly sipping his tea.

"No matter how hard you say you are trying, you're not getting the job done. What are we to do? If you're going to talk like that, then next year we'll also have you do the accounting."

Oh, Toshiko was good! And the following year, Shoko was doing the accounting. When she looks back, Shoko thinks that Toshiko was slowly but surely helping her by increasing her workload. There was really nothing to cry over. But at the time, she was frustrated that she couldn't win Toshiko's approval and sad that she couldn't live up to her expectations.

But the hardest burden to bear was the fact that Toshiko never really understood that the miscarriages weren't Shoko's fault. It was a generational divide. For Toshiko, a woman wasn't really a woman until she had given birth. "What are we going to do with a bride who can't have children," she would say. This would bring Shoko to tears, and she would protest. Yet no matter how much pain she was in or how mad she was at Toshiko, Shoko would never say one bad thing about her mother-in-law. The stress was palpable in the household because Masanobu and his father had both a familial relationship and a work relationship — in the family business, there was only one other employee, and the father was the boss. To keep their relationship on a steady path, a wife was not supposed to bother a husband too much with her concerns. A wife's job is not to fill her husband's head with complaints about her mother-in-law. This was Shoko's policy since they got married.

After many years of the two of them fighting over this or that, Shoko came to realize that while Toshiko may be insensitive, she was a gentle person at heart. She also began to understand that Toshiko had accumulated quite a wide range of knowledge and experience over her long life. Shoko had found herself thinking many times that grandma's wisdom was necessary not only for taking care of the shrine but for raising her children.

For example, once one of the children had a fever. Shoko didn't sense anything abnormal and thought, well, we'll just wait and see. Toshiko urged her quite strongly to take the child to the doctor because she hadn't taken in much liquid. Shoko thought to herself, "What a pain," but she did as she was told. The doctor checked the child, said she was "one step away from dehydration," and quickly prescribed an IV. From that day on, when Shoko grew irritated with her mother-in-law, she told herself, "There's some truth to what the old lady says. I can't just ignore it all."

Shoko also began to understand why it was pointless to say "I'm trying" to Toshiko. When it comes to work, the only thing an outsider cares about is whether you can do the job or not. Working at a shrine meant working for the customers, but it also meant serving the gods. There are certain chores where "sorry, I made a mistake" just doesn't cut it. The only way to advance in Toshiko's experienced eyes was to continue to learn through trial and error. Shoko felt a certain easing of pressure when she realized it was better to go to Toshiko and say, "I'm sorry, but I don't know how to do this. Please show me." This brought out a sort of fatalism in Toshiko, who would think after a certain point, "Telling this woman anything more is a waste." As a result, their relationship had evolved to the place where Toshiko would tell her, "One good thing about you is you're docile. It is something we expected in a bride. But don't be foolishly honest. The world just isn't that nice to fools."

❀

THESE DAYS, when Shoko comes home from her chores, she'll go straight to Toshiko's door and chat with her about her day. "Do you know what happened today?" Then Toshiko will say, "Sit and have some tea," and will listen to Shoko's recounting of the day, prompting her at the proper places with a "what happened next?" or a "really?" Once in a while, she would interject, "You know, life isn't that simple," and then launch into one of those stories that only an older person can tell. The two couples would basically eat their meals separately, but when Shoko was especially busy with the seven-five-three celebrations or the New Year's festivities. Toshiko would come by with a dish and say something like, "I figured you had no time to cook."

And recently, this happened: Shoko had become interested in furs and was secretly looking at them on Internet shopping sites.

One day, she noticed that Toshiko was carrying a fur handbag.

"Wow, what a cute bag. Where did you get it?" Shoko asked.

Toshiko looked her in the eye and said, "So, you want a fur?"

"Yes. They're so nice," Shoko could only respond honestly. Toshiko stared at her for a moment, thinking, then pulled her cigarette case, glasses and wallet out one by one and handed the bag to Shoko. "Here, it's yours."

Without thinking, Shoko said, "Really? OK, I'll take it before you change your mind," and offered her vinyl bag in exchange. "Do you want this one?" Toshiko exhaled through her nostrils in disgust. "Are you crazy? That cheap thing?"

When Shoko went out with her girlfriends, she showed them the bag, and they all oohed and ahhhed over it. Then she'd tell them that she got it from her mother-in-law. "It's not every day that you get a gift that expensive," said one friend. "You must have been very hesitant to accept it."

"I'm oblivious to that kind of thing," Shoko later said. "Toshiko would tell me that's one of my merits. But I'm sure she must have been surprised to have her son bring home a bride like me. Now I am so thankful toward her."

These days, Shoko will often share a secret with Toshiko but not Masanobu. In some ways, Toshiko has become Shoko's most faithful companion and friend. Shoko still makes a mess of things from time to time, but she feels under her skin that she is surrounded by the love of the Omori family.

"I used to have a complex about all my blunders. But my father raised me right and helped my bland personality develop into something more — something deserving of the temple."

Shoko smiles, her eyes wide and innocent, like a little girl.

LONG DISTANCE LOVE

Rina Tanabe, Finance, 24

MARUNOUCHI, Japan's biggest office district, explodes with color at noon as women in their twenties and thirties pour out of their offices and into the area's many restaurants and cafes. While nearby Nihonbashi is dominated by the greys and blues of men's suits, Marunouchi attracts young, fashion-conscious women. In fact, Marunouchi has a long reputation of accommodating more working women than the rest of the city, and the symbol of this reputation is the old Maru Building, now called the Marunouchi Building. Standing in front of Tokyo Station, this building, built in 1923, survived the bombings of World War II and became famous for being the home to many of Japan's "office ladies" or OLs.

Since the reconstruction of the whole Marunouchi neighborhood was completed in 2002, the building has been reborn as a multi-use structure complete with fashionable boutiques and restaurants. It is a temple to the emerging working woman's culture. More women are planning their careers these days, and the idea of women as people who simply help around the office — the OLs — is slowly dying out. Marunouchi is now filled with working women on the career path.

Because of this, the streets are filled with women in smart pantsuits, colorful one-piece dresses or company uniforms, their stylishly coiffed hair battling the wind. Amid this rainbow of colors, Rina, the product of an English mother and a Japanese father, draws unwanted attention because of her deep features and large brown eyes. As many as seventy-seven percent of the twenty-something working women in Japan dye their hair, according to a 2004 survey by the Japan Soap and Detergent Association. Dyed hair is so prevalent among young women that in Otemachi, another Tokyo business hub, young women with black hair are the minority. In this sea of dyed hair, Rina's natural, lustrous brown locks, unaided by highlights or dye, and brown eyes that shine in a way no color-contact could duplicate, prompt passers-by to take a second glance.

When Rina was growing up in Fukui Prefecture, her exotic look was more a burden than a blessing. She grew up gloomy amid the unwanted attention, a child of two countries in an age when that was extremely uncommon. Rina's mom raised her and her two siblings in Fukui, and Rina had the exact same education as the other Japanese children. Though she sometimes spoke English with her mom at home, England seemed a far-off destination to her.

But when she went to elementary school, the other students would tease her. "Hey, speak a little English, OK?" "Are you a foreigner?"

The teasing never escalated to bullying, but Rina remembers worrying about being so different. "I thought about it a lot." At the same time, she says, she had wonderful friends and didn't dislike being with others. Still, she was a shy girl cursed to stand out because of her appearance.

By middle school, the comments slowed, and Rina spent less time thinking about her different appearance. Although she didn't dwell on the subject, she figured she'd lead the rest of her life as a Japanese person, slowly blending in.

In high school, something awoke in her. "If I keep on with this high-school life, nothing is going to change," she remembers thinking. "Every day, I'd go to school and do my extracurricular activities. I suddenly felt that I wanted to do something different. I decided to ask my parents to send me to school in England."

She lived in a dormitory in her English school. Studies proved difficult for Rina at first because her English was limited, but her father had made her promise that if she went abroad, she'd stay at least one year. She worked until she was delirious at times, and after one year, the school felt so much like home that she extended her stay for another year. One year led to another, and in the end, Rina lived in England for about seven years, finishing university there and spending one year in Canada on an exchange program.

During her time in England, Rina realized, "I'm not a half; I'm a double. This gave me confidence. These days, I think beyond the framework of Japan or England. I think that I could adapt to just about anywhere. I'd like to live in a lot of different places. But if I had to choose an identity, I guess I would say I am Japanese."

Even today, Rina still hears people say there's a gap between her look and her character. "I guess they mean a person with my face isn't supposed to be speaking in the Fukui dialect. But I think, why not? That's the way it is."

❀

RINA'S BOYFRIEND, Takashi, is studying in Canada now. Over the three years that they've known each other, it seems that most of their time has been in a long-distance relationship. They met on a university exchange program in Canada, Rina coming from the UK and Takashi from Japan. Rina had little experience with men and was not the type to make a move on someone. "I'm too shy. There is no way I'd do that," she says. She had wanted a boyfriend but never quite had the chance.

"I'd never even had a date," she says. "When I entered high school and then when I transferred to the UK, I kept thinking, 'Will there be someone for me?' but no one ever appeared. The same was true in university. Nothing was happening."

It didn't help that she had an early curfew while living in the dorm. Plus she was busy with homework. There wasn't time for love. In university, she shared a house with others and had all the freedom she wanted, but "people who dated kept changing their partners. Maybe it's that way in Japan, too. People would just meet each other in bars and go home together. I hated that sort of thing. Time passed, and it was time to go to Canada."

Takashi became Rina's first boyfriend when she was twenty-one. When one considers that Rina crossed the Atlantic and Takashi crossed the Pacific, their relationship was off to a pretty dramatic start, but things proceeded slowly. For about six months of their year abroad, Rina saw Takashi as just another guy in the group of Japanese people she had befriended. They'd shop together and go out to eat, but there were no sparks between them. However, one night when Takashi called her, everything began to change.

"It was night. He called and said that there was something he wanted to apologize for. Could he meet me? I wondered what it could be as I went outside to meet him. He came up and confessed, 'I'm sorry. I've grown to like you. Please go out with me.'"

Rina was twenty-one and Takashi was twenty-two. Rina was taken aback by his confession. "I'm sorry. Wait a minute. I never saw you that way," she told him. She figured that Takashi must have thought about this before he blurted it out, but there were only about six months left on their year abroad. "At first, I told him 'no way.' I explained that I hated long-distance romances."

Rina remembers Takashi's reply: "Some long-distance relationships work. If you don't try, how will you ever know? I really don't like to give up on something I have yet to try." It was a suitable reply for a man studying to be an engineer. They continued talking that night, but nothing was resolved.

Rina had still not said yes, yet Takashi kept finding time to meet her in the dorm. They didn't take the same classes, so if Rina wanted to ditch him, she could have. Instead, she went to the movies with him and hung out. He continued to tell her that he liked her, and she kept replying, "Hmmm. I'm not sure."

After this had continued for about a month, Takashi was just about ready to give up.

"When I think back on that time, I was pretty happy. He wouldn't quit and he kept telling me how much he liked me. I wasn't sure what I felt, but I had begun to be attracted to him," she recalls.

Rina finally made up her mind to say yes to Takashi as they walked over a frozen pond in the dead of winter. Takashi, growing numb from trying, said to her, "Tell me the truth. Whether it's yes or no, just tell me how you feel."

"I'm not sure," Rina replied, "but I think I'm starting to like you."

Rina was looking down the whole time. Takashi gave her an encouraging couple of pats on the head.

These new lovers didn't hold hands or hug or kiss on their first night as boyfriend and girlfriend. They just walked across the ice together and returned to their respective dorms.

"Why didn't you say something sooner? I was going crazy," Takashi later asked.

"It took my all to give you that response," was her answer.

❁

IT WAS FAR from a torrid love affair at first. "It was more like a friendship headed toward love," Rina said. The campus was full of couples walking hand in hand, hugging or kissing in public, but Takashi and Rina didn't even try to hold hands.

"I was the one to initiate it, trying to hold his hand until finally he held mine back. I used to wonder why, when he was so bent on going out with me, I had to push just to hold his hand. New couples are often all over each other, right? We weren't like that at all."

Slowly but steadily, the distance between them disappeared. Their first kiss was well after they had started going out, on Christmas morning.

"Can I kiss you?" he asked.

"OK," Rina replied, closing her eyes.

After that, they quickly became more intimate. Takashi didn't get along with his housemate, and before she knew it, he was spending pretty much all of his time at her place. Rina shared a house with two Frenchwomen and an Englishwoman. They also would come and go with their boyfriends, so Takashi was always welcome.

In those days, the young couple would cook and eat and study together. At first, Takashi would sleep in his own bed, but after a while, he was sleeping with Rina nearly every night. These were happy times for Rina. "Those were the days when I slept pressed up against the wall with Takashi in my little single bed."

They were both virgins when they started going out. In the beginning, Rina said, "I left it up to him. The first time, we really didn't know what we were doing. It was painful. I wondered what all the fuss was about. We kept trying and discovering new things. I don't have anything to compare it to, but I think things are going well now."

❦

THEIR HAPPY time together was fleeting. Before long, they both had to leave Canada. They decided to use their last week together to travel. They caught a plane through Seattle to Alaska.

May in Anchorage was cold. They headed to the northernmost settlement on the North American mainland, Barrow. The airport was a little building that looked like a small house with a galvanized iron roof. They exited the building and looked around: a few buildings, restaurants and one supermarket. Rina was excited. It really felt like they had reached the end of the world. From here, Rina would return to England and Takashi would return to Japan. "I kept thinking that soon we would part. We had talked about what would happen, but it wasn't something you could solve by talking, so after a while, we just stopped."

When they parted in Seattle, Rina began to cry. Takashi tried to cheer her up, patting her on the head and saying that they could do it; they could make this work.

Rina returned to England and finished her last year of university. Takashi returned to his university in Sendai. During that year, they saw each other only once, when Takashi and his friend flew to England for a week. The next summer, Rina returned to live in Japan after a seven-year absence.

But even after Rina had returned, she lived with her family in Fukui for the first few months while Takashi was at university in Sendai. "I didn't have any money, and a bus trip to Sendai took overnight. I think I went up there twice to see him."

In September, Rina found a job in Tokyo. She was now a two-hour bullet-train ride away from Sendai. Just when she thought they were getting closer, that winter Takashi decided to do an exchange program in Canada once again so that he could learn from a famous engineering professor.

"I didn't complain. He had made his decision. He wanted to do it for his studies. I didn't cry when he told me, but when I went to see him off at the airport, I burst into tears," Rina said. "I'm predictable. He said, 'Don't cry. What we have is going to continue. Bye bye. I'll see you.' I think it's easier for the one who is leaving. It's painful being the one left behind."

For the long-distance lovers, airport farewells became especially painful. But for Takashi, who loved planes from a young age, it was a little easier: he hoped to be an aeronautical engineer someday. When they arrived at the airport, he'd become animated, explaining to her the wonders of this machine and that gadget. Rina didn't understand the first thing about airplanes, but she felt proud as he talked about the machines that he hoped would be part of his future.

"He wants to build planes. He has a dream and he is working so hard to achieve it. That makes him so attractive to me."

❁

RINA MANAGES product control for a financial institution these days. She majored in mathematics and is working in a department that deals with numerical analysis and calculations. The work is far different from the math she studied in university, and it proved confusing at first, but after a year and a half on the job, she's become accustomed to it.

This is the job that brought her to Tokyo, but for Rina, born and raised in Fukui Prefecture, Japan's capital city remains a foreign land. She had never lived on her own before and had no idea where in the vast cityscape of Tokyo she should look for an apartment. She eventually settled on a neighborhood where a friend from her Fukui school days lived. It's a fifty-minute commute to work, but her place is in a peaceful residential area with a fair amount of greenery, which makes Rina happy.

She awakes at seven and leaves the house by eight. She usually gets home from work at around eight in the evening. On weekdays, she has dinner, watches a little TV and goes to sleep. It's a simple existence. On the weekends, she meets her girlfriends at cafés or restaurants, and once in a while, when she's in the mood, she takes out her camera and shoots some of the scenery in her neighborhood. In the winter, she goes snowboarding with friends.

There are times when she feels lonely. Having lived in dorms and shared houses for so long, coming home to an empty apartment can be tough. "On those days, I take a bath and go to bed. I just tell myself not to think about it. I could call someone, but if I start talking, I think it would just make me sadder."

Rina and Takashi usually talk on the weekends. They use Skype, the Internet phone service, so they don't have to worry about the cost of the call. The time difference isn't a big deal since Takashi is something of a night owl.

"We don't talk about anything specific, but when we do talk, I feel at peace. But sometimes, when I just get tired of it all, I cry. He'll say, 'I want to come see you, but I can't. I'm sorry. I know I'm making you sad, but just pull through this.' In the end, I usually say, 'OK, I'll try.' My friends laugh at me. They say I'm like a child. But for me, this is pretty normal."

Takashi has a year and a half left in Canada. Then he'll come back to Japan. If everything works out, they'll be closer, Rina hopes.

"I really want to get married some day. My friends are getting married and raising children. In Tokyo, people say that I'm only twenty-four, but in Fukui, that is marrying age. When I got to Tokyo and heard everyone talk about how they didn't want to get married, I was kind of shocked. My mother was always a homemaker after her children were born, and that's what I want to be. I want to raise my own children, not hire someone else to do it. Once I have children, I'll probably quit my job. If I can afford to."

While Rina is in finances, Takashi is pursuing a career that could easily take him overseas. No one really knows how long he'll stay in Japan. "I can't worry too much about the future. We just have to try and see how it works out," Rina says, sounding very much like Takashi.

Their current goal is to live close to each other. "That's something we have to do before we think about marriage," Rina says with a laugh. "Long-distance relationships are difficult, but breaking up with Takashi is an even worse option. That's the way it is."

The hem of her coat flutters in the wind as she gets sucked into the bustle of Marunouchi. ❁

ACKNOWLEDGMENTS:

I am indebted to my publisher, editor and long-time friend, Bruce Rutledge, for giving me the support and encouragement to complete this project. This book would not have existed without his continued efforts to bring the project together and his balanced editorial judgment. My gratitude also goes to Yuko Enomoto, who spent so many hours translating most of the transcripts. Her excellent translation and her fine word choices made the transcript much more profound than the original.

I am grateful to our art director, Craig Mod, whose superb artwork gives the book a definitive presence. He also acted as sales/marketing representative in Tokyo and was the cornerstone of our project, providing me with all the necessary logistics as well as psychological support. My thanks also go to Dave Rutledge for his deep insights. His patience while reading and proofing the book gave me the courage to continue on, especially when I felt lost in the details. Although I am responsible for the stories, this book was born as the result of a team effort with everybody at Chin Music Press.

I owe particular gratitude to my sister, Naomi Morishima, who read every single word I wrote since I started this project and gave feedback on each paragraph. I couldn't have done the job without her standing by me throughout the whole process. My thanks also go to Peter Fuchs, who helped me become more honest and see things from different perspectives.

I am also indebted to my friends and their friends, who shared their life stories and their views on sex and marriage, and who connected me with the women I interviewed. I cannot write down all the names here, but you know who you are and how appreciative I am of your kindness and encouragement. This project was not possible without your participation and enthusiasm.

And, finally, my gratitude goes to all the women I interviewed whose names I cannot disclose here due to privacy issues. I cannot express how much I appreciate your courage in sharing your stories with me and readers across the globe.

— Sumie Kawakami

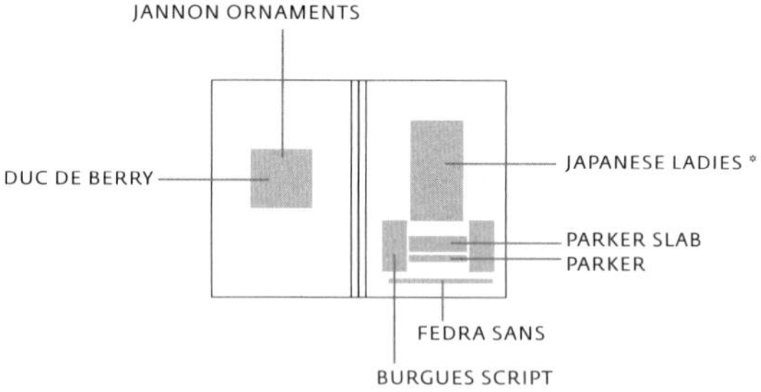

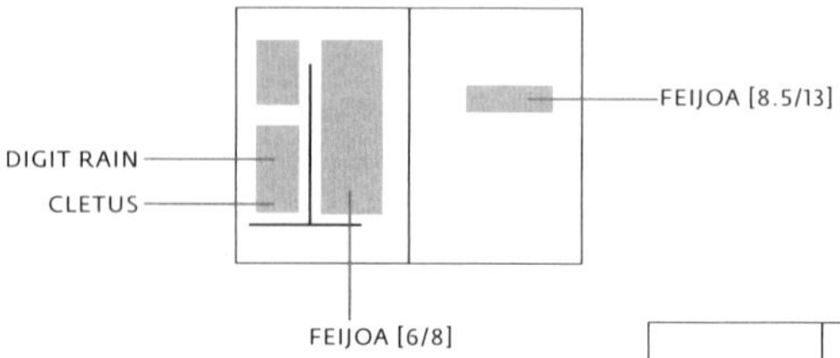

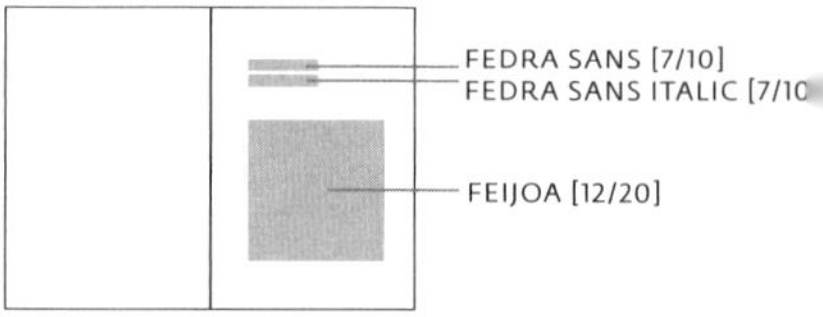

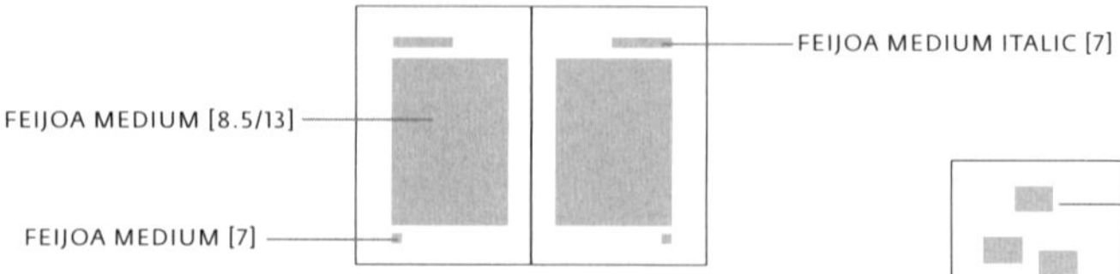

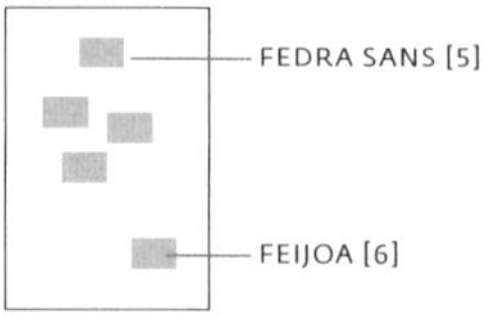

FEDRA SANS	HTTP://TYPOTHEQUE.COM
FEIJOA	HTTP://VLLG.COM
PARKER	HTTP://FONTFARM.DE
JANNON	HTTP://STORMTYPE.COM
ENDPAGES	MEIJI ERA KIMONO PATTERNS
COVER AND TOC	TAISHO ERA WOODBLOCK PRINTS FROM *KOKUSHINENPYŌSAKUIN*

* Cover girls from an old haunt in Jimbōchō. They don't make 'em like this anymore.

c.m.